THE BRIGHTON STORY

Being the History of Paul Smiths, Gabriels and Rainbow Lake

by

GERALDINE COLLINS

THE CHAUNCY PRESS

Saranac Lake, New York 12983

THE BRIGHTON STORY

Being the History of Paul Smiths, Gabriels and Rainbow Lake

Library of Congress Cataloging-in-Publication Data

Collins, Geraldine
  The Brighton Story

  Bibliography: p. 204
  Includes index.
  1. Brighton (Franklin County, N.Y.: Town) — History.
I. Title.
F129.B53C64 1986   974.7'55   86-6829
ISBN 0-918517-08-7

First edition: 1977 North Country Books
Second edition: 1986

A Division of M & M Publications and Sails, Ltd.

Introduction

My hope in collecting this material was to preserve the experiences of our early settlers so that they might be enjoyed in future years. All statements of fact are made in good faith in the various sources of material used. It is not to be assumed, by any means, that this is a complete history of the Town. I am sure there are omissions. Some areas, I know, are not covered because of the lack of recorded facts and the failure of human memories. This I regret. The story could have been complete if all the local happenings had been set down long ago, before so many of our "old timers" had left us.

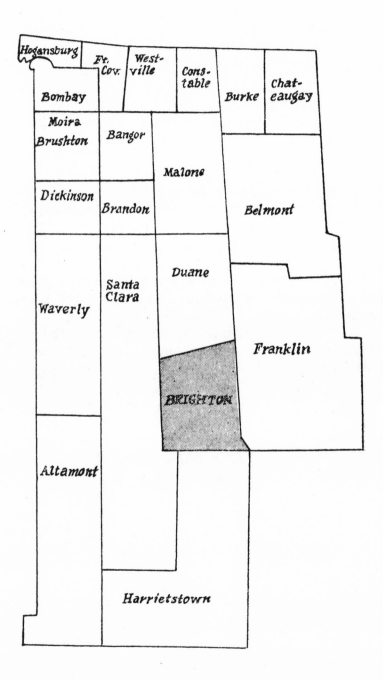

CONTENTS

LIST OF ILLUSTRATIONS

ix

Backgrounds Help Set the Scene

Since the seventeenth century, when the French, Dutch and English missionaries, traders, soldiers, and explorers made their exploits into northern New York, the Adirondack region has had an international fame for its beauty and health-giving climate.

The rugged heights and broad expanses of forests and lakes provide retreats for the game and fish. The vast tracts of virgin land, which the state of New York owns, provides perpetual shelter for wildlife. Although the railroad opened the great North Woods, and the state system of highways has further made all parts of the Adirondack region more accessible, the charm of the primeval forests and mountain scenery still remains.

Visitors and health seekers have been drawn to the Adirondacks from all parts of America and Europe to what is recognized as the most distinctive and natural beauty of eastern North America.

All the land in the Town of Brighton was originally a part of the Macomb Purchase of 1791. Alexander Macomb came from Ireland in the late 1750's and located at Detroit, Michigan. In the short space of 13 years he made a fortune in the fur trade. In 1775 he moved to New York City and married the daughter of William Constable, who was one of his partners in the Macomb Purchase. Even though the price for this four million acre tract was only eight pence an acre, Macomb never consumated the contract for he became financially involved to the point of failure the following year. A series of

1

transfers divided up the land and the various sections went to his silent partners in this deal. This is how William Constable acquired a considerable tract. On his death, his daughter Harriet, who was married to James Duane, inherited a considerable portion of her father's holding in the Macomb Purchase. It was from this tract, known as the Town of Duane, that the Town of Brighton was set apart in November of 1858.

Brighton is a part of Franklin County which lies in the extreme northern part of New York State bounded on the north by Canada with the St. Lawrence River forming three miles of its northwestern border. The Town of Brighton lies in the southern part of the county and has roughly 83.40 square miles with approximately 40% of that being state-owned land.

In the beginning the town was densely wooded throughout, mostly with pine but some hardwood and softwood mingled. The mountainous contours of the land made most of the area unsuitable for cultivation. Some areas have been cleared, but with the altitude of about 1,640 feet, frost is a constant threat to serious aggriculture except for about three months in the summer. The soil is, in general, sandy with a goodly supply of rocks, some pretty large. Within the boundaries of the town are found many lakes; the larger being Osgood, Lower St. Regis, Spitfire, Upper St. Regis, Black Pond, the Spectacles, Barnum, Mountain and Jones Pond (sometimes called Lucretia) and many smaller ponds. It shares Rainbow Lake with the Town of Franklin. There is also the St. Regis River which has its beginning as it leaves Lower St. Regis Lake, and many other small brooks and streams.

The character of the land, mostly wilderness, and the natural resources of timber and game, were responsible for the type of men who came to our area. Likely it was the striving for cheaper lands and a desperate chance to improve their lot that brought them. Most men who did come at this early time faced dire need, very hard labor and at best only a meager living. But come they did . . . mostly from New England, and they were God-fearing, family men. They were men without much education but they had a natural endowment of good judgment, native intelligence and were forced to be enterprising individuals by circumstances. There were not very many people who came to the general area at first but as time progressed it gained a reputation as an ideal recreational center and health resort. In the end, many a business man, tired and weary from the troubles of the city, came here to find comfort and satisfaction in the restful occupations of hunting and fishing.

Franklin County had not grown very much at the beginning of the 1880's and the population of the entire county was not quite 3,000 by 1810. Practically all of this number were those who settled in the northern section, at Malone, Chataguay, Constable, and Dickinson. Growth was slow and it only doubled in the next ten years and each ten following until 1860.

It was in November 1858 that all of Township 18 of Great Tract No. 1 of Macomb's Purchase and the south half of Township 15 . . . a total of 53,760 acres, was set off from the Town of Duane to make the Town of Brighton. It is reported that Brighton took its name from one in England. At the time of its creation the population was about 200 inhabitants. The assessed valuation of the town in 1864 was $39,954. A report for the year 1865 showed a decrease to 160 population. In 1875 the county report indicated that there were 48 dwellings in the town, 22 were frame buildings and 26 constructed of logs. Of these, only three were of value in excess of $2,000; 13 worth less than $250; 16 were valued at less than $100, and eight were placed at less than $50. In this year there were 247 people in the town and most were considered to

3

be natives (born in New York State) but some came from Vermont and a few from Canada and England. Compared with the rest of the county, Brighton that year had the least improved land, 1,504 acres. They produced the least hay, fruit, and other crops, probably because of the type of land. Only 27 so called farms existed then, half of them were under 100 acres. Most of these farms just produced enough to support the family, but early signs of the future potato farming were indicated by the fact that 34 acres were in potatoes in 1874 and the following year that was increased to 44 acres. In 1875, nearly 2,000 pounds of maple sugar was produced, but this was not much compared to the rest of the county. There were 76 milk cows, with some milk going to the factories but 4,000 pounds of butter was made in the homes.

Even at this early date (1875) the town was mindful of its responsibilities, for there were four school districts with seven teachers for the 71 children attending school. It should also be noted that the smallest amount of relief money in the county was paid out in the Town of Brighton.

By 1890 the population had reached 500; the state figures for 1915 give Brighton a total of 741. While the rest of the county has decreased in population since 1940, Brighton has increased 35.8%. The 1960 federal census showed Brighton to have 1,092 and the 1970 figure was 1,473.

The growth of the population in the late 1800's and early 1900 was due to the various health institutions established, as well as to the growth of the numerous boarding houses, not only for health-seekers but also for the sportsmen who came to fish and hunt.. It should also be noted that the railroad made its appearance during this period.

The following table gives an idea of the present-day Town of Brighton:

4

	Acres
Total Land (83.39 square miles)	53,760

Taxable, 1971:

Paul Smith's College	7,318
New York State	21,082
Private	21,560
Total Taxable	49,960

Exempt, 1971:

Paul Smith's College (campus, etc.)	98.50
Paul Smith's College (golf links, etc.)	1,347
Paul Smiths' College (White Pine, Osgood, etc.)	336
New York State Forest and Wild Land....	2,002
Catholic Church	.50
Catholic Church	1
Episcopal Church	3
Presbyterian Church	1.50
4 School Districts	2.75
Town of Brighton	8
Franklin County (right-of-way)	.09
Total Exempt .... (approx.)	3,800

Weather records over the years indicate that practically the same climatic conditions must have prevailed in those earliest days of settlement as we have now. Great quantities of snow, like 1902 when 132 inches fell, and 1911 when 90 inches came before the first of February. Extreme cold in the long winters with some summers bringing little warmer weather or considerable rain while others would be hot and dry. The percentage of sunshine is always minimal. One of the saving graces is the generally dry atmosphere which helps to make the cold seem not quite so cold. Many of the town residents firmly state that despite the five months of sure winter, there is no place, climatewise, they like better.

Early Settlers

The earliest known settlers in Brighton were Moses Follensby, Samuel Johnson and the Rice brothers, Amos and Levi. The exact date when Follensby settled is not known. He is reported to have built a camp about three miles above the Keeses Mill site (which came later). He disappeared mysteriously in 1823. At a very early date this same camp area also attracted Peter Sabattis, a St. Regis Indian, who frequently came for the exceptional fishing and hunting. Follensby gave his name to several bodies of water in our area. In fact, Lower St. Regis Lake was originally called Follensby.

In 1815 Samuel Johnson came and settled on a height of land two miles east of Paul Smiths. Exactly where he built is unknown but it is believed that one of the foundations that can be seen on the country road is the groundwork of his place.

Amos and Levi Rice came to the community either in 1819 or 1820. Levi built his home near where the St. John's Church in the Wilderness is now. He also built a primitive grist mill, which was probably the first industry in the town. Amos Rice went farther north to the area known as McCollom's at the present time. While he lived there he built the Earl MacArthur home and that still stands. A mountain and a pond were named in his honor.

Oliver Keese and Thomas A. Tomlinson came to Brighton in the spring of 1851 and built a dam in the rapids below the outlet of Follensby (Lower St. Regis

Lake), west of the present community of Paul Smiths. Then they built a lumber mill near the dam. At first the business was operated by Keese and Tomlinson but later a Mr. McLean from Franklin Falls came to run the mill. Lumber from this operation was hauled to Port Kent to be used in building ships. This was likely the second business started in the town. Arthur Osgood came sometime before 1850 and tried to farm it about where the old Scout Camp was on the west shore of Osgood Lake.

Another pioneer, James Wardner, came to the region in 1849 on account of his health. He located at Rainbow Lake where he eventually operated a hotel. Shortly after this his brother, Seth Wardner, also settled at Rainbow.

Apollos Smith first came to Brighton in 1858, when he began construction of the log building on the shore of St. Regis Lake that was to develop into the famous Paul Smith's Hotel by the late 1800's.

In some cases Brightons' early settlers came for the especially good hunting and fishing. That certainly was the case for A. A. Smith, whose whole livelihood was dependent on these factors in the early days, and this was the deciding consideration in his making the change from Hunter's Home in Loon Lake. James Wardner is reported to have come for his health, and we know that many others have come in the later years for this reason, but in the beginning years it is doubtful that many tried to survive in this primitive unsettled area with the idea of improving their health. Most who came were attracted by the opportunity for employment in the sawmills or the woods jobs in connection with the mill. After Smith, Wardner and some other hotel keepers began to have increased business, those interested in guiding for a living found good employment available in these hostelries. Then as the wealthy campers began arriving to stay for the summer season, many of the men and women found employment with these campers as caretakers, cooks,

7

maids, boat tenders and other jobs. Gabriels Sanatorium provided some work but the care of the patients was mostly in the hands of the Sisters. Most of the residents of the town in the early 1900's were earning a living in some way either at the hotels or the hotel-related businesses, for by this time the lumber mills were no longer offering much work. A few found themselves operating grocery stores, garages, gas stations, dairy farms, and quite a few were finding seasonal work in the building trades.

Several small communities make up the Town of Brighton. In each case families collected in an area for a specific reason.

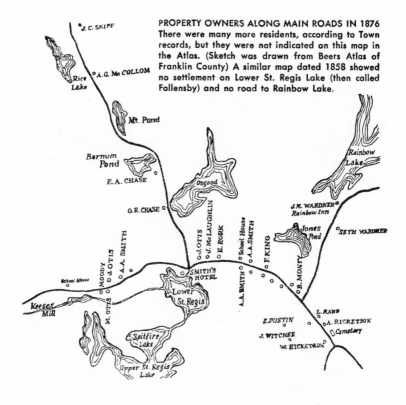

PROPERTY OWNERS ALONG MAIN ROADS IN 1876 There were many more residents, according to Town records, but they were not indicated on this map in the Atlas. (Sketch was drawn from Beers Atlas of Franklin County) A similar map dated 1858 showed no settlement on Lower St. Regis Lake (then called Follensby) and no road to Rainbow Lake.

8

Communities of Brighton

Keeses Mills

In the earliest days, many families were attracted to the sawmill started by Keese and Tomlinson. The company built houses for the settlers and more than 15 families came in the first few years to work in the sawmill. Among the pioneers who settled the community of Keeses Mills were Josuah Otis, John Hall, Henry Hobart (later moved to Gabriels), John Redwood, Irving Jacques, Joseph Newell, John Jenkins and George Skiff. The descendants of these men populated not only Keeses Mills, but have spilled over into Otisville which is located on the same road a few miles closer to Paul Smiths.

A man by the name of Roswell M. Shurtleff who came to the Adirondacks to write and draw pictures of the region, made his headquarters at Keeses Mills in August of 1858. He boarded at the home of mill manager, Tom O'Neil. He described O'Neil as being of large physique and good hearted. Tom used to enjoy taking the rim of a barrell, or the back of a chair, between his teeth and raising either to a horizontal position, claiming that it made his jaws feel good.

Mose Sawyer, an old time guide, lived in Keeses Mills most of his life and in his later days ran a store in his home. He had five children, so has many descendants in the area. Joshua Otis fathered a large famliy that moved up the road a few miles toward Paul Smiths into an area that became known as Otisville. Josh's son, Fred, owned the house where Martin Lyons lived for many years. An-

9

other son, Myron, lived just south of the Raldy Martin home. Al Otis settled where Herb Lyons lived in later years. James Betters and his wife came from Ausable Forks to Otisville and raised a family of fifteen. They ran a store for many years right in their home. Jim had a peddler's cart that he ran some of the time, going between Otisville and Gabriels. B. A. Muncil, the contractor, had his fine home and business in the Otisville area.

Paul Smiths

There is really no such thing as a village of Paul Smiths. It is purely a post office address of the area surrounding the Paul Smith Hotel. Actually there are not too many homes involved. It is mostly the hotel area that developed into the community at Paul Smiths. In connection with the hotel there was a general store that sold everything from building supplies to food and clothing. In later years the Hotel Company provided the electric service, the telephone and telegraph service for the entire Town of Brighton. Paul Smiths was the center of business for a large number of people even though there was no individual private enterprise involved. It was entirely the Smith family operation that gave employment to guides, waitresses, woodsmen, cooks, gardeners, dairymen, clerks and storekeepers.

With the passing of the hotel days, the college has assumed the same roll — that of being the center of employment for the town. Only now, those employed are in somewhat different occupations. Now the community is growing because of the influx of faculty and administration families as well as student families who come to live here during their college days.

In the early days, when Wardner's Inn was popular, what we call the county road was a narrow, sandy thoroughfare and there were several families that lived along

10

there in log houses. Several were from the Otis family. John Otis, whose wife was Lucretia (sister of Phil King), once lived where the Town Hall is now. A son, Frank Otis, married Jennie Wallace and they started housekeeping on the back road but later moved to Easy Street where Jennie spent the rest of her life. She was Town Clerk for many years.

Easy Street

The part of town known as Easy Street developed in the period after 1890, for the most part. In 1890, there were only two houses on the hill. One was at the foot of the hill, about where the Town Hall is now and was built by a man by the name of Goodspeed. A bit later when Orman Doty's father burned out on the Jones Pond road just beyond there, the Doty's moved into the Goodspeed house. The only other house at this time was the John Rork place at the top of the hill where Ben Martin lived until recently.

A brook crossed the road at the foot of the hill and the only way to get across was to ford it in a shallow place in the early days, according to James Wardner's journal. This brook was called Weller Brook and it was some time before it was properly bridged. The brook gained its name for Tom Weller, a guide for Paul Smith, who bought some land near the stream for his home.

It was a bit after 1890 that this settlement grew because it was so close by and handy to Paul Smith's Hotel. It was here that stage-coach drivers and the guides who took out the hunting parties for Paul Smith built their homes. As they saved enough money to establish a home they bought land all up and down the hill and built neat, comfortable cottages, each with its own garden. The men worked mostly during the season when the hotel had guests in need of transportation and amusement. They

11

were relatively well paid, according to the pay scale of the time, guides receiving three dollars a day according to Stoddard (1905), giving them more than enough to live over the winter. This feeling of security was noted by the men and they felt they were on easy street, so the name, applied in jest, has stuck to the area to the present time.

Others who built on the hill about 1910 are Bill Titus (R. Fountain), Ed Slavin (H. Brulliea), Jim Titus, Sr. (Jim, Jr.), Frank A. Otis, and Jennie Otis (Lepine).

The next place was Phil King's farm. It was located a bit beyond the top of the hill on the west side of the road. (This was known as the Military Road at that time.) This had started as Paul Smith's farm with Phil running it, but the little Frenchman, Philemon King, was so enterprising that Paul made a bargain to sell the farm to Phil. The agreement made, allowed Phil to pay for the farm with milk, butter, eggs, and vegetables. The prices agreed upon were to remain fixed, regardless of the market price, up or down. Phil carried an account book with him when he made the deliveries to Paul so that entries could be made in his record. Nothing much is left of this once busy farm, except some lilac bushes, and a few apple trees. Phil had a large hall on his farm where square dances were sometimes held. It was also a polling place at election time.

Across the road from the King farm was the school house, which was built at this early date. According to the school records on file in the Town Hall, the school opened in 1871 with 14 children, and the teacher was Melifsa Goodspeed. This was the school that Orman Doty attended as did the Smith boys, Henry, Phelps and Paul.

Next to the school, on the same side of the road, was the Methodist Church, built in 1893. The church was built through the interest of Mrs. Paul Smith who took charge of raising the funds, even though she was a Presbyterian herself. After the church was closed up, the hotel took over the property, making it into a residence occupied at one time by William Stalker who ran the sawmill operation for many years for the Hotel Company. It is presently used by the College faculty.

There was a log house where Bill Fletcher now lives and Halsey Brulliea remembers living there as a very young boy for a year (1905). This burned and the frame house replacement also burned.

In the early 1900's Jute King lived where John Helms does today. Jute was a meat dealer and had a market in his home. The Saranac Lake *Enterprise* reported on May 18, 1913, that "Jute Q. King completed a very fine country home of fourteen rooms with hot water heat and a cobblestone fireplace." Jute was the son of Phil King, and was County Welfare Commissioner from 1913 to 1930.

The Harold Martin home was once known as the Bon Air Cottage where Mr. and Mrs. George B. Riley took guests (circa 1916) from May 15th to October 15th at $2 a day or $9 a week. They could take as many as ten guests according to a New York Central Railroad folder of that year. Mrs. Riley had also gained quite a reputation as an artist and her pictures were well known locally.

Phil King's daughter, Kate, married Walter McDermid, who stayed to help Phil on the farm. Walter also had a milk route on the St. Regis Lakes.

Gabriels

The settlement around Gabriels was first called Brighton back when there was only the Rands and Ricketsons and most of the families were nearer to the Split Rock area. The real community of Gabriels came about as a result of the building of the Adirondack & St. Lawrence Railway in 1892. Prior to the coming of the railroad

13

there were a few homes of guides and the farms of those who did some farming along with their guiding. But it was not a community with stores and a post office. There did not seem to be any particular reason for a village to start here, yet it did and in about 20 years developed into quite a settlement. A number of families came with the workers building the railroad, but only Charles Downs and his wife stayed after the workers left. Mr. Downs had come from Ellenburg.

By 1910, in addition to the Gabriels Sanatorium, there were two stores, a small hotel, a garage, and a blacksmith shop, and a saloon. The railroad had a station here and for several years this was the point of arrival and departure for most of the visitors to Paul Smith's Hotel, who would leave the train here and travel to the hotel by means of a short stage trip. The railroad station was known as Paul Smiths until 1902 when the name was changed to Gabriels Station.

Gabriels had a population of about 200 people by this time, and a reputation, even then, of having more than its share of saloons.

The first store in the village was reported to have been built by David Sterns about 1892. It was a clothing store located on the main road. B. A. (Barney) Lantry, who came to work at the Sanitorium, operated a store in an old building in the back part of the San property. When the land was sold to the institution he moved down to the main road and built a store that was later known as the Riley Store. This was in 1898 and Al King ran it for a while and then Charlie Riley, a young man of 22 years, came to clerk. Pretty soon Lantry decided he couldn't make a go of it and sold out to young Riley who continued to run the store until 1950. This was a general store where the customer found clothing, nuts and bolts, wash tubs, plow points, and paint, as well as staple food items. After Mr. Riley died, the store closed and the building

14

went into serious disrepair. The College acquired the property and tore down the buildings in late 1969.

Lantry had also built a blacksmith shop next door to his store.

At one time there was a saloon attached to one side of Riley's store. This was run by a Mr. O'Donnell who had a bartender named Dave O'Brien. Old-timers relate stories of some great fights that took place there. When such a fight got started it went on all day and way into the next day, maybe, with the men throwing everything in sight, from kegs to furniture. The sheriff at that time was Ed Dustin who lived in Bloomingdale. When the roughhouse got too bad, someone would send for Ed. As soon as he got there in his attempt to quiet things down, he'd be persuaded to take a few drinks himself and pretty soon they would load him back into his cart, slap the horse, and Ed would be on his way back to Bloomingdale. Then the fight would resume until it just wore itself out. Mr. O'Donnell was not very well and his children would often go over to Jones Pond and hunt for leeches which would be placed on his neck in an effort to reduce his blood pressure.

Little Zeb Robare had built a log building that served as his home and also a hotel. Known as the Robare House it was located on the corner of the main road and the Rainbow road, across from the Riley store. This came into use in the period from 1890 to 1910.

Robare's had a daughter known as Mag, who often accompanied Zeb on his hunting and fishing trips. She became a guide eventually, a thing unheard of in this country. She was considered one of the mountain characters and after World War I always wore men's clothes. Little Zeb and his wife, Melina, were busy in the hotel with the people who came to Gabriels to visit patients at Gabriels San. Besides the hotel, he was a guide for the William Parker family of Forestmere, near McColloms, now known as Fisher Camp. Earlier he is reported to have been a guide for Teddy Roosevelt. He also operated a saloon in his hotel.

Charlie Riley eventually bought the property and remodeled it into a three-story building with 65 rooms. An early morning fire on October 22, 1941, started in an adjoining ice house and spread to the main building and destroyed the rambling frame Riley Hotel. Fortunately, no one was in the hotel at the time as it had just recently changed from a year-round operation to a summer only operation. The remains of the foundation can still be seen as the building was never replaced. Some fame came to the hotel during prohibition days for it was the headquarters for the state troopers.

Near the Riley store, and almost across from the troopers in their headquarters, was a garage owned or operated at various times during the 1915 to 1930 period by Russ Studders, Leland Chase, Halsey Brulliea, Irving Davis, and Clarence Newell. It was a legitimate repair shop but one of their repair jobs was the installation of heavy duty springs on cars that were in the business of "rum running" from Canada to the United States. Carrying a heavy load, the car with ordinary springs would show it and could easily be spotted by the patrolling officers. Sometimes the garage would be empty of cars at closing time in the evening, but 12 to 15 vehicles might arrive and depart during the night for an exchange of Canadian beer and whiskey. Some of the cars went back north for another load and others scattered ir all directions making deliveries. This operation made it easy for the three saloons in Gabriels to be well supplied with these scarce items. The wooded countryside made it most difficult for the feds. With so many hiding places the officers were hard-pressed to enforce the prohibition regulations.

One of the most colorful of the Gabriels saloons was the one run by Bert LaFountain in his home just a few doors from the Riley store. It was possible to find refreshment here all during the prohibition period as the "friends of Bert" would collect of an evening to visit. He was caught once in a while and cheerfully paid his fine. Even after prohibition was repealed he continued to operate, but without a license. He could have gotten a license, but he just preferred not to. A folk song was written about him and it is still being sung today.

The song was recorded by Marjorie L. Porter, Nov. 15, 1949, from the singing of Mrs. Elizabeth Smart of Redford, N. Y. It is believed to have been written by Dorothy Sequin, who wrote it while traveling with Bert.

Bert LaFountain's Packard

It was on a Sunday morning I headed for the North,
The road I often traveled while riding back and forth
I crossed the old St. Lawrence going straight to Montreal
With Bert LaFountain's Packard and a load of alcohol.

I loaded her with liquor, stocked her with wine and ale
To get across the border I knew I would not fail
They signaled me with flashlights, and wished me to halt
But I tore right by the custom house with LaFountain's alcohol.

The troopers and the immigrationers they soon took my heed
I was rolling eighty and putting on the speed
I was rolling straight to Merril, heading straight for Malone
The word got ahead of me, it was by telephone.

I saw the troopers' barriers and a car across the road
I quickly left the wheel, the Packard, and the load.
It's now I'm out on bail and I know I lost the load
I'm waiting for my trial with it to come next fall.

(above version supplied by Lee Knight, folksinger)

By 1910 a William Goldberg had built a store across from Riley's on the main road. He did not keep it very long, selling it to Lawrence Rafferty who ran a grocery there for many years. In the same store Jack Slattery had his barber shop. Later this was a bar operated by Lloyd Symonds and more recently a restaurant and bar called the Leaning Pine.

Jacob Hyman started a clothing and dry goods business in Gabriels about 1922, in what was later known as the Legion Hall. He kept his store until his retirement in 1943. Both Hyman and Sterns sent out peddler carts in the immediate area. Ike Sterns, son of David, was the one assigned to take the Sterns cart on the road. The Sterns' clothing store was about across the street from Hyman's store.

Albert Premo built a garage on the main street about opposite Rafferty's store in 1925. He rented it to the town for their machinery and trucks after he gave up running a garage. It was torn down about 1960. Another garage was built in 1930 by Earl Martin across the road from his house on the main road.

Between Rafferty's store and Martin's garage there was a novelty store that started up in 1920. Charles Riley built the building but Jenny Flynn ran the store, selling novelties, mostly to the Sanatorium patients who used to walk down to the store. This same building with a bit of remodeling was where Glenn Bacon opened his grocery store in April, 1935. Mr. Bacon had been coming into the area with his meat wagon since 1925. He had made regular trips from Dickinson through Keeses Mills and Easy Street prior to opening his store in Gabriels. His store became an IGA grocery of exceptional quality, catering not only to the local people over the years but to a large number of the summer families of wealth on the lakes. It was destroyed by fire in April, 1969, and was not rebuilt.

18

Just prior to 1900 the Waite Lumber Company set up a portable sawmill near the railroad station in Gabriels. They stayed for one year only. There had been a forest fire on Jones Hill and while the trees had been killed by the fire they figured that the hardwoods logs would be usable for lumber if they were cut right away. Many thousand feet of lumber was salvaged from the injured trees in this way.

About 1920, B. A. Muncil was doing such a large contractor business that he needed a sawmill. He built it on the road to Rainbow about a mile from the center of Gabriels. This mill was under the direction of Con Meagher, his son-in-law. It was here that logs were made into lumber that was used in constructing many of the famous camps on the St. Regis Lakes, for example, the world-famous Post Camp. A bad fire damaged much of the machinery in the mill in November of 1948 and work in the mill tapered off after that time. It finally ceased operation in the late '50's. Brainstorm siding, used on so many Adirondack buildings, is supposed to have been invented here.

The New York Central Railroad Station was located on the north side of the Gabriels settlement. Originally it was a two-story building with living quarters on the second floor for the station master. Walter Andrews lived there for many years in this capacity. The station burned August 22, 1927. It was replaced but on a lesser scale. After the railroad was abandoned, that also was removed.

As the year 1970 rolls around, all of these various business ventures are gone. The Riley store and apartment building was torn down by the College, which now owns the property. The Sterns store still stands but it is in very poor condition, not being used; the Hyman store, later the Legion Hall, is standing, being used for storage by owner Lee Martin. Scott's poultry farm that was so active from 1934 to 1953 in the sale of fancy turkeys,

19

chickens and eggs, is no longer in business. At this time there is only one gas station, one bar, and a small lunch-room-bar combination.

Even though the land is hilly and stony, some hardy farmers in the immediate area have succeeded in making the sandy land productive. Arthur Leavitt, Douglas Martin and Frank Hobart had made the start and William Leavitt, David Young and the Tucker brothers, Mark and Don, have continued to make a success of growing seed potatoes that find a ready market on Long Island and other places. Originally these carloads of potatoes were shipped by train, but in late years, with the trains gone, huge tractor trailers do this job. Truck farming to some extent in a small way, was successful by others who sold their surplus vegetables to the summer campers. For a while in the '50's Mr. Hobart shipped a considerable amount of this type of produce to the New York City market in iced trucks, but this is no longer done.

Rainbow Lake

James Wardner, the pioneer settler of Rainbow Lake, lived that first year in a rough shanty that he built beside the brook that ran into the lake. Rainbow was a lovely lake and it received its name because of its shape. In those first few years the living was hard and he kept himself alive by hunting and fishing. James, his brother Seth, and their mother, Phoebe, made up the household, as they cleared some land for their crops and later buildings. In 1858 James married Delia Marshall and built himself a larger and more comfortable home where they began to take hunters and sportsmen who were now venturing into the less settled parts of the Adirondacks. This dwelling soon became known as Rainbow Inn and for many years was a select and preferred resort for sportsmen. The fact that James was a good hunter certainly did much for

20

the popularity of the hotel. The story goes that his wife was a good taxidermist and filled the place with all kinds of birds and animals.

The guide books of 1880 said that Rainbow Inn could accommodate 50 people, with rates being $8.00 per week. If you came by stage to Bloomingdale, they would meet you there. Later when the train was brought through the Town of Brighton, there was a railroad stop just a few hundred feet from Wardner's. The train helped promote his inn in their brochures as early as 1894. The Adirondack & St. Lawrence Line carried glowing stories of Rainbow Lake and this advertisement brought more people to the area. We think of fish stocking as a modern conservation practice, but records show that trout were stocked in Rainbow as early as 1888.

James Wardner built a dam at the head of Rainbow, flooding land enough to take in three natural ponds. For weeks he cut logs and collected big stones. Then when winter temperatures made good thick ice, he hauled the logs and stones onto the ice. In this way he made a dam that, when spring came and the ice melted, settled into place. This way deep water was backed up to make his end of the lake more desirable. Garondah was another property that benefitted from his engineering job.

One of the guests that stayed at Wardner's was the artist, A. F. Tait. He was one of the earliest painters of the Adirondack scene. His fame is greater now as historians, in making a study of his works, have found an excellent portrait of life in our section in the early days. One of his paintings was of the Wardner cabin showing the beehive on the flat part of the lean-to roof. Alongside of the building was a ladder to be used to get up to the hive. This was the actual practice, keeping the hive on the roof, and away from the bears who might come looking for the sweet honey. The ladder was for James to use when he wanted some honey.

21

The Rainbow Inn property, enlarged to eight buildings and several extra small buildings such as barns, boathouse, ice house, and machinery building, was later sold to the Independent Order of Foresters and operated as the Rainbow Sanatorium. When the San was opened on July 20, 1910, it treated its members suffering from pulmonary tuberculosis. It had 600 acres, fifty of which was lake, another fifty cleared land and the rest in woods. In their statement of opening they boasted of being located one eighth of a mile from the Rainbow Station, on the Adirondack Division of the New York Central Railroad. This Sanatorium was in operation until the early 1930's.

Along the road 300 yards farther west, on the same side of the road, was the Garondah Cottage that was built about 1892 by Herman Prellwitz and his wife, Louise (daughter of James Wardner). Their son, James, still lives in Rainbow Lake. This establishment was built on the highest point of land in the immediate area and about 200 feet from the lake. When Louise was left a widow, she married Fred C. Toof and they continued to run the business. It was not as large a hotel operation as the Rainbow Inn. Later the property was purchased by William Prellwitz and was the summer home for the family for many years until it was sold to C. E. Collins, who operated it as a fishing lodge until 1961 when the present owner, John Neronsky, bought it. The original building has now been remodeled so that there is no resemblance to the first Garondah Cottage.

The next property along the same side of the road was built by Leland Chase, probably about 1900. After Chase was killed in a railroad crossing accident at Butt's crossing, just up the road a bit, the house was sold to John Rochester. Mr. Rochester had come to the area in 1912 as a steward for the Forester's San. The family operated it as a summer boarding house for many years.

22

After the San closed, Rochester became a carpenter and did some guiding before he died in 1950.

By a careful search of the pine woods across the road you can find the remains of the foundation of another boarding house type hotel that was called *The Brighton*. This was in operation under the direction of L. R. Morris in the early 1900's. Their advertisement offered accommodations for 35 guests with all modern appointments, including hot water heat, with electric bells in all rooms and lights by acetylene gas. They claimed to have their own garden and a table well supplied with good food and first class service. A further attraction beyond the good house and beautiful scenery was local and long distance telephone in the house and eight mails a day . . . all this for $10 to $15 a week. The Brighton, which burned to the ground in August, 1914, while the owners were at the County Fair, was never rebuilt.

Beyond the junction of the county road, a school house was built as a branch of the Gabriels school. This is now being remodeled into a home. Just beyond this, at one time, there was a store in the gully. For a short time the post office was in this store.

After the sale of the old Rainbow Inn, Mrs. James Wardner conducted a boarding house at Buena Vista Cottage, which was about a half mile farther along the road to Gabriels. This was a quiet homelike resort that boasted of open fireplaces, pleasant rooms and a good home-supplied table. They suggested that guests take advantage of their carriages for rides as well as using boats and guides for hunting and fishing. Buena Vista was purchased by the Orman Doty's in the fall of 1914 and they began operation in the summer of 1915, calling it Rainbow Cottage. They continued to take guests until 1966, when Orman was 84 and Mrs. Doty 82. This cottage is not on the main road today as the highway route was slightly altered in the later years.

Just beyond Buena Vista, part way up Jones Hill, the Frank M. Wardner's (first son of James) also took summer guests in a boarding house type of establishment, according to Stoddard's guide of 1904.

The 1913 New York Central map of hotel accommodations lists Lake Lily Cottage, open in the summer for guests and located on Lake Lily. Nowhere else have references been made to Lake Lily, but apparently it was a name given to Jones Pond at one time. D. F. Bryant operated it about this time and next came Willard Smith as owner. The establishment was more recently known as Pine Lodge. Vere and Emma Mix rented Pine Lodge from Willard Smith in 1934 and finally bought it in 1941. They had a good business going with fishermen coming year after year until they sold it in 1951. It has changed hands several times since then and is presently closed. This place was slightly more than a mile from the Rainbow Railroad Station and then, as now, is considered to be the end of Rainbow Lake settlement.

On the eastern side of the Rainbow railroad station (burned 1934) a farm was built that was connected with both the Rainbow Inn and the Sanatorium. The farm was acquired by William Hogan about 1934 and the family still owns it. Francis Hogan, now Postmaster, has the Post-office and lives in one of the homes on the property. Across the street from the farm is a house that for many years belonged to Art Higgins and for several years the post-office was in the little house beside the main building.

McColloms

The community of McColloms developed around the property of Amiel C. McColloms, who came there about 1849. When he first came the area was called "the burnt land" as it had been burned out for several miles around.

The structure he lived in was the log one originally built by Amos Rice, located about eight miles north of Paul Smiths corner on the road to Malone. Amiel farmed it quite a bit, and also did some hunting and trapping. After a while it gained the reputation of being a pretty good place to get nice fish and venison meals, and since hunting and fishing was good, he built up a small guest business. He became known as Uncle Mac and folks liked to go there but the road was not too good so it was a hard trip, being nearly 30 miles south of Malone and quite a run from Paul Smiths. The accommodations were pretty simple but the folks who did get there had a good time, for Mac took special interest in making sure his guests had the finest sport available.

Clarence A. McArthur, who was the next proprietor, came there in 1873 to take charge of Mac's hop yard and the farm in general. Soon he went into the hotel business with Mac. None of Mac's children had lived very long and when Uncle Mac began to get feeble he gave up all control of the property to McArthur. Under McArthur's direction a new hotel building was put up and other improvements were made so that it soon became a fine summer resort by early 1900 standards. It gradually catered more and more to just plain vacationers rather than hunters. When C. A. McArthur died in 1913 it was found to be very much in debt and was sold under mortgage foreclosure. The creditors sold it to Colonel William C. Skinner but the property eventually came back into McArthur hands when C. A.'s son, Earl McArthur, bought it back. Although Earl was an educator by profession, he ran the summer business for several years. It has since ceased to operate as a resort under the present ownership of Dr. Robert Brown.

Early Homes and Living

The earliest homes were made of logs, carefully chinked with moss and mud, but in most cases these were replaced by frame construction since there was plenty of lumber available with the many sawmills in the area. By mid-1870's the dwellings were about equally divided between frame and log construction. Each home would have its own sewage and water system. Human waste was taken care of by an outside privy, usually in a small building set apart from the house, and later of course by conventional plumbing inside the house. Wells and springs were used for a clean water supply wherever they could be found. Good water was hard to locate in the Easy Street and Gabriels area and still remains a problem today.

There were two areas where people built their own water supply system, other than the one at Paul Smith's Hotel. B. A. Muncil had one in Otisville and James Wardner had one for the Rainbow Inn. Wardner dug a ditch at least five feet deep in order to put his water line below the freezing point. They even tunneled under the roots of big trees, rather than disturb them. They removed ordinary stones in their path and blasted out, using gunpowder because they had no blasting powder, the ones too big to move or go around. The pipe was a series of logs hollowed out with a tool they had devised, and they joined the line together with some special iron couplings. The man who prepared the logs took over two months to bore enough for the half-mile run from the spring to the house. The Muncil project also made use of logs and must have taken much longer to complete, for that one connected many houses over a longer distance.

Judging from the style of architecture, most of the homes were constructed from about 1890 to 1910. Many of these fine old properties built around the turn of the century are still in use. The Quarters home and most of Easy Street, John Helms' place, Leavitt's and Young's in Gabriels and Betters and Crary on Keeses Mill Road are typical examples of these homes while the Orman Doty home and Charles Vahsen's are examples in Rainbow Lake.

Most every home had a small garden to supply the family with fresh vegetables in season and for drying and canning for the winter needs of the family. If they were lucky, they might have some extra to sell to the campers on the lakes. Venison and fish provided some of the meat but after the earliest days they became a seasonal treat for the conservation game laws prevented taking fish and game except at specific seasons. Cows, chickens and pigs were normal for each household.

When the railroad came, it brought in outside supplies so that the Brighton housewife was able to have the same supplies as any household would have elsewhere. Rabbits were hunted for both fur and food; wild bees provided honey for the taking, maple syrup and sugar were made each spring to help satisfy the family sweet tooth, and wild berries and fruits added to this part of the family diet. Apples were scarce as the trees did not do well in the cold climate.

Sickness was an occasional visitor to the area such as in 1918 when the Spanish Flu was reported to have caused more deaths than World War I. Scarlet fever was active in Gabriels in 1902, and showed up again in the winter of 1912, 1917, and 1918. Diphtheria hit the Easy Street School in 1917, but in general the health problems were not too serious. In fact, the climate was considered so good that the two sanatoriums boasted of its power in their advertisements.

Doctors from both sanatoriums provided their services to the local residents and there was always a doctor in Bloomingdale in the early days. At present, Saranac Lake is the health service center with its fine hospital and many doctors.

Like today, each home had its own medicine chest. Castor oil was a stock item as was collodion (composed of equal parts of ether and alcohol) used for burns and small wounds. Flour and salt paste would stop the flow of blood. Mud was good for bee stings. Various ointments were made from the fat rendered from animals and mixed with tar or camphor. Whiskey was a standard medicine for almost anything. Leeches were popular, for a while, to control blood pressure.

Big events of the year were the Malone Fair, held each August, the Saranac Lake Winter Carnival and the championship skating races also held in Saranac Lake. Most social life was confined to the town. It was common to have a square dance in one's home, and Wardner's, McCollom's and Phil King's places were the favorite spots for these parties. Sometimes a whole group would arrive at someone's home for a party as a complete surprise, with the women all bringing food enough for everyone.

Trapping was popular among the men as a method of earning some cash money. Before the snow came the men would set out their traps in the likely spots where they thought the animal would be traveling. Some serious trappers would have a trap line, which was a long series of traps over great distances. In this case, it would take the trapper several days to cover his line, checking the traps for animals caught and resetting sprung traps. Fox, bear, beaver, mink, sable, and other animals provided fur and food as well. Trappers carried a supply of food from home that might consist of jerked venison, biscuits, maple sugar and, if they were gone for several extra days, they might shoot a rabbit to stretch along the food supply.

Many of these skins were sold but some were used in the home. One hide that was popular in the home was buckskin. They used to soak the hide in lime water. After a week or so, that would loosen the hairs so they could be scraped off easily. Then the side could be stretched over a smooth log and the real scraping operation began. When it was clean and smooth they would work oil into the skin. Many leather items like gloves could be made from the finished hide.

Old Time Guides and Guiding

Earning a living by guiding was no easy job, in spite of the name "easy street" that was tagged to their way of life. A guide was either employed by a hotel for the season and re-let by them to the guest camper who requested this service, or a guide might operate on an independent basis with the camper making his own deal directly. In either case, the guide ordinarily furnished the boat and simple cooking utensils, did the work involved in taking the party around, either fishing or hunting, or sightseeing; did the cooking, and carried the boat and duffle if a portage was necessary. Almost all guides had Adirondack guideboats and were good at using the oars, making the boat skim along the water with ease. They often took trips with parties that lasted from a few days to weeks, traveling the waterways and following the carries of the St. Regis chain of lakes as well as the Saranacs, or down into the Fulton chain of lakes. They would camp at night in a lean-to, or occasionally stay at a hotel along the way. Since the camper-guest came to stay all summer, there was plenty of time for him to truly enjoy the woods, mountains and streams. Such a camping party would normally consist of two people in a boat plus the guide and the equipment and supplies. Of course, several boats and guides might travel together in a party on such a trip. For all this service the guide was paid about $3 a day according to Stoddard in the 1903 edition of his book, *Adirondacks*. That is not very much by today's standards but it was considered to be a better than average day's wage at that time.

The number of guides that were reputed to have made their headquarters at Paul Smiths varies from 50 to 100 and almost any guide worth his salt did work for Paul at one time or another. Stoddard in his 1880 book gave a list of many of these guides, some of whom are well-known in local lore. For example, there were:

John Hall	Ben Monty	John Otis
Henry Martin	Sylvester Newell	Erwin Jaquish
Lovell Newell	Fred Otis	Elbridge Ricketson
Albert Otis	Elverdo Patterson	John Rork
Sylvester Otis	Frank Robare	James Cross
David Robare	Zeb Robare	Jacob Hayes
Ben St. Germain	Joe L. Newell	Fred Martin
Henry Weller	Moes St. Germain	Ed Noyes
Thomas Redwood	Ed Corbin	Myron Otis
George Martin	Frank Hobart	Ed Dustin
Lias Hall	Doug Martin	Oren Otis
Phil King	George Moody	Moses Sawyer
John McLaughlin	Loney Moody	Will Titus
	Joseph W. Newell	

Some guides on Easy Street had permanent jobs at the camps on Osgood Lake and the St. Regis Lakes. In a sense they were camp caretakers but they also did "tripping" with the summer visitors and guided the hunting and fishing parties in spring and fall. Among them

30

were Abram Swinyer (Durkee Camp), Justus Quarters (Drake Camp), Charlie Bigelow (Dr. Baker Cottage at Paul Smith's Hotel), Seth Lyon (Townsend Camp), Douglas Martin (Godfrey Camp), Sanford Hayes (Cameron Camp), Bob Newell (Dickenson Camp), and Will Titus and Ed Slavin had similar situations.

These camps were large and, although built in a rustic manner, luxuriously furnished. Lots of entertaining was done during the season so many servants were employed and one or more guides. Guides were always busy in the summer months but in the fall after the wood was cut for the next year and the ice house filled, there was not much for them to do except to keep the roofs shoveled. This had to be done once or twice, depending on the winter. No wonder they had leisure time to play cards. The story goes that a certain group on Easy Street would often play all night and sometimes all day Sunday.

Because of the growth in the travel of these campers over considerable distances of waterways, with portages frequent, the Adirondack guide boat is believed to have been created for this specific use. This is the belief of James Wardner, who also was a guide as well as a hotel keeper. Many canoes were used at first but the guide boat was like no other boat. It was very light, weighing only about 50 pounds including the oars. It was a beautiful, slender creation; strongly built of thin spruce or cedar and carefully varnished. It looked something like a canoe but was moved and guided by oars in fixed locks. People found it easy to carry on a shoulder yoke.

All guiding was not the routine trip. Sometimes the sports were not used to being in the woods and that left the guide with everything to do from trying to keep the sports from falling overboard, to doctoring their insect bites. Most of the men, once they got used to the woods life, would do their share of carrying duffle on the portages, guiding the boat sometimes, helping with the cook-

31

ing. Guides could make stews and do some other simple cooking, but nothing fancy and stews got pretty tiresome to the long trippers, so many of the sportsmen came prepared to do some of their own cooking. The camp fire was used for cooking and that was an art in itself.

There were two methods of hunting in the early days of Brighton that are completely illegal today. It was considered perfectly alright to hunt deer with dogs, and dogs were specially trained for this purpose. Old time pictures of hunting parties included many of these dogs, in some cases each on a chain and controlled by a guide. When hunting was done at night it was often done from a boat, with a "jacklight' 'affixed to the front of the boat. This was a basket-like contraption made of metal and mounted on a pole that hung out over the water. Pine knots or pine cones and cotton, or something similar, would be set on fire to give light. This same jacklight was used in fishing at night with the idea that the light attracted the fish as well as guided the fishermen. Hunting with dogs was the first method to be discarded and made illegal. The real sportsmen preferred to·sit on a watch spot and let the guide go noisily through the woods in an attempt to drive the unsuspecting deer toward the waiting hunter, much as hunters do today.

JAMES CROSS — Came from Morristown, Vermont, and went to work for Paul Smith, April 5, 1866, as a guide. Aside from guiding, he made fishing rods that he sold for prices as high as $25.00. He also made boats. He seemed to have a natural talent for mechanics and one time made a telephone. Once you met him you could never forget him because he was a towering 6 ft. 3 in. in height and lean as could be. One year he and Phil King (5 ft. 6 in.) went to a convention for assemblymen. They were introduced as the "long and the short of Brighton." James was married to Albertine Hall, daughter of John

Hall of Keeses Mills. He served in the Civil War and survived to tell many stories of his experiences. He died on April 18, 1908, of pneumonia and is buried in St. John's Cemetery.

LORENZO CHASE — Guided for James Wardner at Rainbow Inn.

JOHN McLAUGHLIN — Lived on Easy Street with his daughter, Mrs. Jud Quarters. He guided for Paul Smith from 1858-1887 and his wife, Mary, worked some of the time at the hotel as a domestic.

MOSES SAWYER — Came from Canada at the age of 15 and in 1864 guided for Paul Smith. He had no education when he arrived and Mrs. Smith taught him along with her son, Phelps. He guided Edward Livingston Trudeau.

WILLIAM H. TITUS — Began his guiding career at Paul Smiths at the age of 17. He was a nephew of Paul Smith. When he was interviewed in 1937 he recalled that things were all different back 30 years ago. Then you brought along a side of salt pork and some flour for hot cakes and you stayed in the woods until everyone in the party got a buck. It was nothing to carry a 25-pound pack basket and walk 20 miles a day.

SYLVESTER NEWELL — Famous guide for Paul Smith, died in 1918.

HENRY MARTIN — Lydia M. Smith's brother, and son of Hugh, was guide to Teddy Roosevelt when Teddy visited Trombley camp as a boy. He was also an excellent riverman for logging. He became Superintendent of the Trombley Camp as well as chief guide. Mrs. Trombley was a Vanderbilt and the camp—Pine Point—was located on Upper St. Regis. The architectural style of the camp was Japanese. It was later sold to the Pratt's.

ERWIN JAQUIS — Guide. Also a Civil War veteran. Died 1915.

HENRY HOBART — Was guide-caretaker for the Penfold Camp on Upper St. Regis for many years, but kept his farm on the side.

CHARLIE BIGELOW — Moved to Easy Street from Bloomingdale. At one time he guided at McCollom's Hotel for the fishing and hunting parties. He would drive the eight miles from Easy Street to McColloms in a horse and buggy. One day while driving along the road, about half way there, he saw a partridge in the road up ahead. He stopped the old horse, but instead of getting out of the buggy, he stood up and took a sight on the bird getting ready to shoot it. Just then the old horse, curious as to what Charlie was doing, and why they had stopped, turned his head to see, and Charlie shot him right in the head.

ORMAN DOTY—Rainbow Lake guide who was chosen to be Calvin Coolidge's special guide during his stay at White Pine Camp in 1926.

Government

When the Town of Brighton was set off from the Town of Duane in November, 1858, James M. Wardner was Supervisor of Duane, and at this time he automatically became the first Supervisor of Brighton, since he was already a resident in the Brighton area.

The Supervisor, from the earliest days, was the main town officer, responsible for whatever government action was considered necessary. At first the Supervisor was elected annually and in the Town of Brighton the town officers met only once a year in a formal meeting. Only after 1889 was any mention made, in the records, of more than one meeting a year. After 1901 the term of office for the Supervisor was extended to two years.

The first order of business of the town, according to minutes of these early meetings, was the raising of monies to support highways and bridges. The amount raised at first was $250.00 annually. This same amount seemed suitable for about ten years more. Then it was raised. Five districts were created and all the inhabitants along these highways were liable for, and assigned to work on their particular district road. Some land that belonged to William Ricketson was apparently used in a road improvement program and the Board voted to pay him $25 an acre for what they used. This was in 1866.

During the Civil War a town recruiting officer was needed and A. A. Smith was the one named responsible for getting the two men needed to fill Brighton's quota.

After highways, the next matter for consideration for the town was a burying ground. Apparently there was considerable controversy over where it was to be. After 1867 for several years there were resolutions passed to have it first one place, then another. Finally, in 1878, it must have been settled, for the order was passed to stake out the various lots in the grave yard, and in the following year money was raised to paint the fence at the William Ricketson grave yard. This is the present Town Cemetery that has the name *Mountain View* on the entrance gate.

A March, 1896, meeting raised $70 to lay iron pipe from a spring on the F. Weller farm to the highway. A few questions put to old-timers revealed that this piped water was to provide refreshment for the horses who traveled the highway.

An interesting outcome of the 1897 meetings was to allow liquor to be drunk on the premises where it was sold and it also approved the off-premises consumption, selling for medical purposes, and selling by hotel keepers.

One of the ways that road improvements were made was by the men contributing their labor. There were some who preferred to work and others who wanted taxation of everyone to pay for the roads. Very likely those who favored contributing their labor found that easier than finding the hard cash to pay taxes. This problem was constantly under debate, switching from one side one year, to the other side the following year. Taxation finally won out in 1899 and was used from then on.

A most important decision was made in 1900 by the Town Board when they granted "An exclusive right and franchise to erect, construct and forever maintain an electric light system" in the town; plus a telephone system; plus a telegraph system. This went to Paul Smith, of course.

In 1909 the first indication that increased business of the town was making it necessary to have frequent meetings and that the town officers were spending so much more time on their duties that it was being considered a necessity to pay them a salary. To this end the Supervisor, Town Clerk, and Highway Superintendent were asked to keep an itemized record of their time for one year so as to have a base for their salaries. This was also the year they voted to spend not over $500 on building a shed for the town machinery. It was to be 20 feet by 70 feet and B. A. Muncil was to build it.

Scarlet fever raged through the town in 1912. The Board called on the Town Health Officer, Dr. F. M. Nobel, to take whatever action was appropriate to control the epidemic, and this included quarantine power. Cost for medicine and medical attendance was assumed by the town. It was reported that Tyler's, White Pine Camp, and Alexander's were bad off, so many in the family ill. A total of $250 was raised to pay the help in these scarlet fever cases.

At first, the hall on Phil King's place was used for voting and meetings. This was located about opposite the early school house and the Methodist Church, on the right hand side of the road going toward Gabriels. When Walter McDermid, his son-in-law, took over they continued to use the hall but in November, 1912, he informed the Town Board to look for another place to hold meetings and elections.

A committee was appointed to consider locations and plans. Soon after the first of the year they voted to raise $3,000 for a hall. However, it was not until June, 1914, that the Board accepted the lot offered by Phelps Smith, situated at the intersection of the Gabriels and Rainbow Lake road, known as the John Otis corner. The size of the lot deeded to the town was five and a half rods on the Gabriels road and running back nine rods northeast on the Rainbow road. B. A. Muncil was entrusted to make up the plans and specifications. When the bids were opened the low bidder was George Trombley but he did not show up on the date set to sign the contract so the contract was finally awarded to Mr. Muncil. An additional $350 was voted to put in a vault to store important records. This has proved to have been an excellent investment for the town has safe storage for old records and in most cases these records are still intact and available for research. Many inquiries come each year to the Town Clerk and the Town Historian and this file of back records is the answer to most of these queries. A phone was installed in the hall after it was finished.

Compensation insurance for the highway employees was adopted in 1917 by the Board.

For several years the elimination of the Butt's Crossing (railroad crossing on Gabriels-Rainbow Road) took up a considerable amount of the Boards' time. This railroad crossing had been the scene of fatalities, the most recent of the time being that of Samuel Martin and his wife on August 6, 1918. A formal petition was made to the Public Service Commission in 1929 and the Board attended hearings in Malone in 1930 and 1931. The overhead crossing was the direct result of this effort by the Board.

At first all the town banking was done in Malone but the November, 1930, minutes refer to borrowing money from the Saranac Lake Bank.

From the first, highways were a major consideration of the Board and that problem is still with us today. Around 1900 it was equipment like the iron road roller that had outgrown its usefulness so they traded it along with a road scraper and a snow roller for a steam roller. Next they considered a stone crusher and finally decided to get an electric one and installed it on the Mose Russell farm (on the Hobart road).

By 1928 the highway expenses estimate for the year was $14,000 and that was the year they decided to buy a Sargent snow plow.

In this day of inflation it is hard to believe how low salaries were in the '30's, but these are a few of the ones mentioned: Town Clerk—$40.00 a year. Highway Superintendent—$5.00 a day and he did not work on a year-round basis; laborers earned a maximum of forty cents an hour, while truck drivers got fifty cents an hour, top wage. A truck driver was on call in the winter at a flat salary of $100 a month (December-March). This, of course, was for snow removal. With the depression in full swing even this little income was more than welcome.

The town voted $3,775 for work relief purposes (used for road repairs) in connection with the Federal Temporary Emergency Relief Act. Work was done on the Keeses Mills road mostly, improving the banks and curves, but some was expended on the Gabriels-Rainbow road at the railroad underpass area. Welfare problems became increasingly troublesome during this period and

WPA projects were used to relieve some of the unemployment. Late in the 1930's such a WPA project eliminated the curve below Meagher's Mill and another at the Keeses Mill school area. An average of $2,000 was borrowed each year to finance this home relief, until about 1943. The various towns paid all welfare costs at this time.

The voting machine was purchased in September, 1936, and the town adopted the use of the U.S. Standard Voting machine system.

The Town Board voted to place an Honor Roll at the Town Hall which would list those boys who went off to serve in World War II. This was made of wood and put in place in 1943. As the list became longer and longer they soon ran out of space and the project was abandoned. Later, in 1945, the present monument to the war dead was purchased, and the names engraved on it.

A complete list of the Supervisors and the terms they served are as follows:

James M. Wardner 1859-1862, 1864-1867
Appollos A. Smith 1863, 1868-1875
C. E. Martin 1875-1883
Henry B. L. Smith 1884-1890
Phelps Smith 1891-1892
James M. Wardner 1893
Euclid C. Pine 1894-1897
John Carrier 1898-1901
Clarence H. McArthur 1902-1908
Charles J. Riley 1909-1923, 1934-1935
Richard J. Longtin 1924-1933
Cornelius F. Meagher 1936-1941, 1948-1950
Earl T. Martin 1942-1947
Arthur Monteau 1950-1963
Clement E. Collins 1964-1971
Stanley Tyler 1972-

Politically, the registration of the residents of the town had been predominately Republican, from the first years; and in about the ratio of three to one recently. However, there have been several Democrats who have won the Supervisor's spot on the Town Board (C. H. McArthur, Charles J. Riley, Earl Martin and Clem Collins). The Republican party was just newly formed at the time of the Civil War and some of those who joined it were not above changing their minds when the circumstances warranted it. Apollos Smith was a classic example of this . . . he used to brag that he could change politics overnight. And he did have to change constantly in order to keep his Postmastership over the years.

Reports of the Firewarden for the Town of Brighton were recorded in the early years in the New York State Forest Commission Reports. In the Report of 1892 George D. Knowles, Firewarden, states that on June 14, a fire started on lot No. 66, from sparks from a burning house occupied by A. Doty. It burned across lots 67 and 68, and involved two or three hundred acres. Not too much damage was done as it was an old fire slash. On June 15 a fire started on lot 76 of unknown origin. On June 16th a fire started near the Smith Hotel. We used grub hoes, axes and some water.

By 1910 there was a fire observation station operated by the state, located on St. Regis Mountain. The station was installed in April of that year, but there was no tower at this time. There was a telephone line strung the three miles to the station and the observer then was George F. Brown. You could see 12 miles to the east, 15 miles to the south, 30 miles to the west, and 15 miles to the north. It was a most popular climb to the summit and the splendid view made it most worthwhile. A thousand fifteen made the climb in 1924. For many years Lee Martin was the ranger on the mountain, and he was followed by Carl Farrar. Presently the state uses air reconnaissance to spot forest fires and there are no rangers in the tower. People still make the climb to see the view, however.

40

MINUTES OF THE FIRST TOWN BOARD MEETING — TOWN OF BRIGHTON

March 2, 1859

"We the board of inspectors of elections in the Town of Brighton of the 1st annual town meeting held in and for said Town of Brighton, County of Franklin, State of New York, on the 12th day of April, 1859, do certify that the following officers were duly elected to wit:"

Supervisor ....James M. Wardner
Town Clerk ....Alphonso A. Rand
Assessors ....William B. Currier, Thomas O'Neill
Inspectors of Elections ....William Ricketson, Joshua Otis
Justices of the Peace ....John Redwood, Lorenzo D. Rand,
James M. Wardner, A. C. McCollom
Collector ....Joseph Reynolds
Overseer of the Poor ......William B. Ricketson, Lorenzo D. Rand
Constables ....Joseph Reynolds, Thomas Perlman,
Joshua Fuller, William Otis
Sealer of Weights and Measures ....George Ricketson

"This first meeting was held at the home of Julius Quarters, and the following resolutions were passed:

1. Raised $250 for support of highways and bridges.
2. Raised $15 for buying revised statute.
3. William Ricketson was to be overseer of Highways in District 1.
4. Joshua Otis to be overseer of Highways in District 3.
5. Thomas Perlman to be overseer of Highways in District 4.

Signed: A. A. Rand, *Town Clerk*
John Redwood, *Clerk of Polls*

Town of Brighton — Register of Electors
Voters of 1859

Abbott, John
Abbott, Wesley
Bigelow, Dexter
Bigelow, John
Cobb, Jugh
Conger, Henry
Currier, William B.
Douby, Joseph
Douby, Rinly
Fuller, Joshua
Goldin, James
Parker, Captain
Perlman, Thomas
Quarters, John

Quarters, Julius
Hall, John
Hayes, John
Jaquis, Benjamin
King, Philimon
McCollom, A. C.
Manning, Gabriel
Miller, Horton
Noble. Levi
O'Neill, Thomas
Otis, John
Otis, Joshua
Otis, William
Ronalds, A.

Ricketson, Charley
Ricketson, George
Ricketson, John
Ricketson, William
Rand, Alphonso
Redwood, John
Roberts, Harvey
Rork, Edward
Tanner, James
Wardner, James
Wardner, Seth
Weller, Freeland
Weller, Henry
Wilcox, Herman
Williams. George

Board of Registry: Herman Wilcox, Julius Quarters, John Ricketson

Town of Brighton Assessment Roll—1859 (first one)

McCollom & Currier ....600 A.
John Ricketson ....200 A.
William Ricketson ....app. 3,000 A.
Joseph Reynolds ....60 A.
Henry Farrington ....47 A.
William Otis ....30 A.
Lorenzo Rand ....100 A.
Alphonso Rand ....107 A. and 92 A.
H. Wilcox ....106 A.
James Wardner ....100 A.
Annis Weller ....179 A. and 68 A.
Julius Quarters ....100 A.
Edward Rork ....100 A.
Thomas O'Neil ....50 A. and 155 A.
F. or T. W. Curtis ....100 A.
John Redwood ....50 A.
Ambrose King ....20 A. and 99 A.
Norton Miller ....50 A.
Henry Conger ....50 A.
Joshua Otis ....58 A.
S. E. Manning ....90 A.
B. Jaquis ....51 A.
Erastus Kelley ....64 A.
Apollos A. Smith ....50 A.
(valued at $200; military tax 50c; total tax $3.40)
Oliver Keese ....6,971 A. and 1,102 A.

1861 Jury List — Brighton

A. C. McCollom, Burnt Ground (McCollom's) .... Farmer
William B. Curran, Burnt Ground (McCollom's) .... Farmer
John Redwood, Keeses Mill .... Farmer
Thomas O'Neil, Keeses Mill .... Mill Foreman
George Williams, Keeses Mill
Henry Conger, Keeses Mill
Joshua Otis, Keeses Mill
A. A. Smith, Follensby Road (Lower St. Regis) .... Innkeeper
Edward Rork, Quarters neighborhood (Easy St.) .... Farmer
Julius Quarters, Quarters neighborhood (Easy St.) .... Farmer
James Wardner, Rainbow Pond .... Farmer
Lorenzo D. Rand, Ricketson neighborhood
Alphonso Rand, Ricketson neighborhood
William Ricketson, Ricketson neighborhood
Nelson W. Ricketson, Ricketson neighborhood
John Ricketson, Ricketson neighborhood

Dated July 1, 1860

James Wardner, Sup.
Alphonso Rand, Town Clerk
John Redwood, Assessor

Cemeteries

The earliest cemetery was established at McCollom's with the McCollom family plot which was later given to the town about 1884.

At one time there was a burying ground in back of the old Weller home where some soldiers who were killed in the war were supposed to be buried. This was right next to the school house and the Methodist Church. The bodies in this place were moved to the Town Cemetery about 1898 when the highway was changed. Each family was responsible for moving their own people. Orman Doty recalls this difficult task for, as a lad of 15, he helped one family.

Minutes of the Town Board meeting of March 5, 1867, first mentioned buying land from Quarters and Wilcox for a public burying ground. The area was to be square, fenced with cedar and painted white. The following year's minutes made no mention of this, but another vote was passed to spend $65 on buying and fencing one half acre at the Harkness place. At the meetings of 1871 and '72 other resolutions were passed and further proposals were made, but there did not seem to have been anything really settled. It was not until 1878 that the Ricketson grave yard was ordered to be staked out and fenced. This was the beginning of the present Town Cemetery that was given the name of Mountain View.

From the beginning considerable care has been taken to keep the cemeteries in good repair and well fenced. As early as 1889 the Town Board appointed someone to take charge; the first one being George Knowles who "was made responsible for the burying ground in the east end of the Town." At this time the Board stipulated that all persons living outside the town, and wishing to bury in the yard, should pay ten dollars for a lot. Later it was decided that only town residents could use the grave yard. No further mention of the caretaker position was made in board meetings until 1940 when they resolved to hire a man from May to October at $70 monthly. At this time they also purchased a horse-drawn mower for $40. Jerry Hourihan served as caretaker for many years followed by Eugene Drake and recently the position is held by Charles Martin. Additions to the original amount of land have been made and a storage house built. The mowers are now modern gas-propelled riding ones and the best of care is taken to keep the grounds looking beautiful.

Another town cemetery is at McColloms. It was originally a family burying grounds for Amiel McCollom that was given to the town. It is a very small cemetery and has been used mostly by the McArthur's and McCollom's.

A third cemetery was established next to, and in connection with, the Church of St. John's in the Wilderness. Originally this was considered to be the place where the elite were buried and many of the early pioneers of the Adirondacks are buried there. Paul Smith and his family are there as are the Edward L. Trudeau family.

War Records

Records of the participation of men in the armed forces during the Civil War are not very complete but apparently there were about eighteen men who served. This figure was given in Seaver's book, *Historical Sketches of Franklin County*. However, only fourteen names were found in the records in the town vault. The fourteen, and their service record, are as follows:

Bigelow, Dexter Anson	Served 1 year, died of typhoid fever in Frederick Hosp.
Cream, Henry Orin	Served 4 mo., discharged because of disability.
Ford, John	In many battles, returned alive.
Jaquis, Erwin	Was discharged Dec. 14, 1863
Otis, Henry	Served 5½ mo., shot on guard duty at Petersburg and buried there.
Otis, Silvester	Served in many battles, wounded but returned.
Otis, Carre Clark	Received an early discharge, mental condition.
Ricketson, Charles	Discharged after 6 mo., disability.
Reynolds, Joseph Hazwell	Early promoted to Corp., was a Bull Runn, Antietom and Fredericksburg, returned alive.
Skiff, George Hasper	Still in service at close of war.
Wilcox, Alanson K.	Discharged in 1865, remained to live in Richmond, Virginia.

Weller, Henry Gardner	Served 3 years, moved to Hartford, Conn.
King, Cereal	Enlisted Jan. 1, 1864; discharged July 13, 1865.
LaBounty, Simeon	Enlisted Mar. 30, 1865; discharged Aug. 28, 1865.

Soon after the official declaration of World War I on April 6, 1917, various groups were organized to lend war effort aid. A county war chest was formed in July, 1918, and Charles J. Riley was the representative from Brighton. Quotas to be raised were assigned to each town, Brighton's share being $3,185. Considerable publicity was put out to convince the population that this was a safe agency to take care of the distribution of funds to various war service organizations such as Red Cross, Jewish Relief, Armenian, and Near East Relief. None of the towns in the county met their quota but Brighton did as well as any of the others, for it raised $716.28.

Feeling ran high, against the Germans, all over the country and this area was no exception. The booklet, *Franklin County in the World War,* reports that: "At Gabriels, several persons of German ancestry were in the habit of meeting at a certain house for the purpose of rejoicing over Allied reverses. An impressive warning was given that the practice must be stopped and the mistress of the place was made to take a picture of the Kaiser from the wall and cast it into the fire." This story was part of the Vigilance Committee report.

Brighton exceeded their quota in the War Savings Stamp program and was awarded an honor flag.

Local efforts to raise money during World War II consisted of card parties galore. Every club seemed to be having these parties on a regular basis and a considerable amount was raised in this manner. The local 4-H group raised $374 at one party for the Christmas fund for service men in 1944. This same club also collected scrap paper and rags for the war effort.

Service Roll of Honor — World War I — Town of Brighton

Name	Entered	Age	Branch	Organ	Discharged
Blanchard, Frank	5/27/1918	25	Machine Gun	2nd Anti Air. M.G. Bat.	3/7/1919
Benware, Harrison	5/27/1918	29	Machine Gun	2nd Anti Air. M.G. Bat.	2/10/1919
Blanchard, John H.	7/21/1918	24	Infantry	Co. C, 348 Inf., 87th Div.	3/20/1919
Bryant, John V.	12/12/1917	31	Air Service	349 Aero Sq.	12/23/1918
Bryant, Percy D.	12/12/1917	23	Air Service	224 and 141 Aero Sqs.	7/9/1919
Barnes, Frederick W.		25	Navy		
Brulliea, George Halsey	8/12/1918	23	Air Service	Texas	5/20/1919
Downs, Arthur J.	5/27/1918	26	Signal Corps	326 Field Sig. Bat.	7/3/1919
Longtin, Richard J.	5/27/1918	30	Infantry	Co. B, 2nd Pioneer Inf.	7/9/1919
Lyman, Clarence H.	1/3/1918	24	Quartermaster	Quartermaster at Large	7/3/1919
Lyons, Herbert F.		26	Infantry	Supply Co., 2nd Pioneer Inf., 207th M.P. Co.	1/7/1919
Leavitt, Charles I.	5/27/1918	29	Med. Corps	37 Ambul. Corp., 6 San Tr.	
MacArthur, Gladys	1/1918	30	Y.M.C.A.		8/1919
Martin, Randolph S.	2/8/1918	22	Air Service	14th Balloon Co.	4/23/1919
McDermid, King S.	1/3/1918	23	Mortor Trans. Corp.	Co. A, 8 Reg. Div., Mort. Sup. Tra.	2/8/1919
MacDonald, Archibald K.	5/27/1918	32	Infantry		6/10/1919
Otis, Oscar J.	7/13/1918	20	Motor Trans. Corp.	707 Motor Trans. Co.	6/14/1919
Otis, Howard	8/15/1918	21	Engineers	Co. H, 2nd Eng. Regt.	12/18/1918
Otis, Roy A.	5/10/1918	27	Machine Gun	Co. B, 146 Mach. Gun. Bat., 5th Div.	Died 12/2/1918 of wounds r'c'd in action
Ormsby, Archie B.	10/23/1918	23	Infantry	2nd Co.	12/27/1918
Paye, Bernard L.	8/30/1918	30	Army Serv. Corp.	6th Reg., Coast Artillery Corps, Battery H	2/18/1919
Riley, Thomas F.	5/29/1917	24	Artillery	57th Mach. Gun Bat., 19th Div.	1/22/1919
Russell, Edward H.	8/26/1918	30	Machine Gun	Co. B, 12th Ammunition Tran.	2/1/1919
Sawyer, Jerry E.	8/7/1918	23	Artillery	Co. A, 10th Eng. Forestry, AEF	2/7/1919
Sawyer, Frank H.	8/14/1917	23	Engineers	Co. I, 59th Pioneer Inf.	2/13/1919
Strack, Harry L.	7/21/1918	24	Infantry	149th Aero Pursuit Sq.	7/8/1919
Sussey, Christopher A.	10/5/1917	30	Air Service	Headquarters Co., 50th Inf.	3/19/1918
Tebo, George S.	11/4/1909	28	Infantry	U.S. Army Hosp. No. 41	1/27/1919
Ziegler, Lillian Oliver	10/24/1918	30	Res. Nurse Corp.	Battery A, 13th Reg. F.A.R.D.	4/13/1919
Rork, Spencer J.	9/9/1918	21	Artillery	1st Co., 151 Depot Brigade	1/2/1919
Paye, Harry A.	10/5/1917	27	Infantry	Co. C, 5th Train. Bat.	11/3/1917
Newell, Harold J.	7/1/1918	22	Signal Corp.	N.Y. Wagoner Army	1/23/1919
Muncil, Benjamine A.				Pvt., Co. A, 12 Ammo Tr. N.Y.	
Muncil, Madison				Pvt., Co. A, 2nd Anti Aircraft	
Tucker, Joseph J.					

Unfortunately, no such record was kept of those who served in World War II, and no record seems to exist at the county level either. The following list was compiled from the headstone information of those buried in the cemeteries in the town and from a clipping scrapbook kept by Gladys Blanchard.

Service Roll of Honor — World War II
Town of Brighton

Abare, Donald F.
Abare, Eugene L.
Abare, Lawrence E.
Abare, Sydney
Benton, Roger
Benware, Emery
Betters, Stuart J.
Blanchard, Earl H.
Blanchard, Ralph
Block, Joseph E.
Brulliea, Hubert E.
Buckley, George H., Jr.
Buckley, Lockwood F.
Carr, Robert A.
Catchman, Charles E.
Collins, Clement E.
Connors, Karl F.
Connors, Walter J.
Crary, Lloyd
Crary, Harold
Crary, Newell
Crary, Vernon
Davidson, William B.
Davidson, William G.
Davidson, James R.
*Drumm, Kenneth B.
*Farrisse, Helen M.
*Farrisse, Harold E.
Farrisse, James V.
Farrar, Carl, Jr.
Finlayson, Arnold R.
Flanders, Robert C.
*Flynn, John J.
Fountain, Clayton K.

Meagher, Neil F.
Mose, Edgar
*Muller, Clayton F.
Muncil, James M.
Muncil, Robert A.
Muncil, Robert D.
Murphy, Hollis E.
*Newell, Harold Lovell
*Newell, Loren C.
Odell, Charles
Otis, Joshua
Otis, Kenneth N.
Perrino, Henry
Quain, Lawrence R.
Probert, Tharon Tyler
Redwood, Leon
Riley, Charles
Riley, James J. B.
Rochester, Paul G.
Rogers, Philip R.
Rork, Charles A.
Rork, Clarence A.
Rork, Philip J.
Rork, James R.
Sawyer, Charington F.
Sawyer, Ernest J.
Sawyer, Gordon
Sawyer, Glenster F.
Sawyer, Leo C.
Shackett, William C.
Shanty, Leon
Simpson, Charles W.
Slavin, Edward H.
Smith, David E.

48

Garvey, Leo F.
Goodman, Francis A.
Gallagher, Robert A.
Gonyea, George E.
Hourihan, John A.
Jaquis, Marston
Jaquis, Martin
Jaquis, Robert A.
Kelly, James R.
Kenny, Michael A.
Kirkbride, James B.
LeMay, Earl T.
LaMay, Harold J.
LaMay, Louis H.
Lester, Albert E.
Lester, Raymond F.
Lester, Vaughn H.
Martin, Earl W.
Martin, Harold E.
Martin, Leander J.

Smith, Peter
Stern, Henry H.
Stern, Muriel
Stern, Zelma
Stern, David B.
Sweet, Tim
Sweet, William L.
Sweet. William N.
Symonds, Clarence E.
Symonds, Lloyd J.
Titus, William, Jr.
Traynor, Harry S.
Traynor, Lawrence G.
*Traynor, Raymond N.
Tyler, Gordon E.
Tyler, John H.
Vivlamore, Richard D.
Vivlamore, Robert E.
Wheeler, Oscar L.
Wilson, Ralph J.
Yelle, Wilbur F.

---

* Died in service.

Korean veterans are likewise unlisted, but Benjamin Martin and Charles L. Skiff are known to have served.

Two of our Brighton boys were killed in action in Vietnam at about the same time. Both Vaughn Doty and Howard Paquin received military funerals and are buried in the town cemetery.

Transportation

In general, between 1855 and 1890 all means of communication and transportation was dependent on the stage-coach. All travelers were carried by the coach as was the mail. Even the news was relayed by the driver and his passengers along the route traveled. The driver knew everyone along the road and he carried messages, delivered parcels, brought medicine to the sick and the

49

cheer of friendly gossip to those who seldom saw anyone else in the remote areas.

Most of the drivers were good-natured and kindly. They had to be skilled in handling horses, usually four to six in number. Their work demanded a certain inner cool for they often faced dangerous situations, and they became hardened to fatigue and exposure to all kinds of weather. Roads, many of them corduroy, were at best narrow, rough and full of pot holes. In wet times they were a sea of mud and when dry the sand ruts were enough to try anyone's patience. No thought was given to making roads without curves and there was no machinery to eliminate the steep grades. Roads sort of took the line of least resistance, so to speak, for they were made to run over the easiest trail possible. Drivers were lucky to make thirty to forty miles a day and often they had to finish a trip after dark.

Only one round trip a week was possible from Port Kent to Paul Smiths, because of the very poor road conditions. As roads became better and when a road was made connecting Bloomingdale to the Military Turnpike near Ricketsons corners, it was possible to make two round-trips a week. It was necessary to change horses both going and coming, and since the Franklin House at Franklin Falls was a mid-point, this was done here. This also gave the travelers a chance to have their noon meal as well. Fitch O'Brien drove this stage for about 12 years, using four horses as a rule, but when the roads were muddy, he increased his horsepower to six. Passengers used long coats and covered their heads with hats and veils to protect themselves from the elements and the inevitable dust when the season was dry.

Of the two most widely known drivers, one was George Meserve, who was on the coach operating out of Paul Smith's Hotel. George was born in New Hampshire at Conway, in 1834, inheriting his father's love for, and

50

knack of handling horses. He drove a baggage wagon during the Civil War at General McClellan's headquarters on the Potomac and was later with Burnside and Hooker, and finally with Grant at the fall of Richmond. In 1878 he came to the Adirondacks and started driving coaches for Fitch O'Brien, already famous as a driver. Soon after this he went to Smith's and for 12 years drove the familiar six-horse Concord Coach for the Hotel. He was an expert with horses and took great pride in putting on a real show for the passengers. One of his tricks was to let the horses take it real easy for several miles back from a scheduled stop so that he could make a final burst of speed as he would pull up to the hotel. He had a pair of white buckskin gloves that he would don for this final burst of speed. Sometimes he would also announce his arrival with a thundering blast on the coach horn.

The story goes that the famous showman, P. T. Barnum, suggested to Paul Smith that he acquire six matched white horses for his stage line to use on the last part of its run from Plattsburgh. Paul liked the idea and was delighted with the results. It was a most impressive sight to see that newly painted and varnished coach draw up to the hotel with those six white horses. George Meserve also liked the show he made and was always ready to add some little touches of his own. The white horses were kept at Loon Lake and they only made that part of the run, both going and coming.

The summer that President Grover Cleveland spent in the area he was much impressed by George Meserve and when he left he took George with him as his coachman. George Meserve died in 1905 at Ticonderoga.

Stages lines flourished in the area until the Chateaugay Railroad extended its narrow gauge line from Plattsburgh to Saranac Lake in 1887. Rainbow had a station on this line located about four miles from the Rainbow Inn area. This was considered to be close enough and it

51

was not difficult to send a stage to the train for guests. People were not too eager to have a train real close because of the noise, smoke and fire danger from sparks and dumped ashes. Trains started many forest fires by dumping hot coals along their tracks.

The main stage coach routes of the early days started from Elizabethtown, Keeseville and Ausable Forks. The Whitehall and Plattsburgh Railroad was built to Ausable River Station as early as 1868 and this instantly became the distribution point for passengers and freight for our area. From Ausable Forks, the stage went through Black Brook to the Toll Gate, where they could take the Port Kent and Hopkinton Road to Loon Lake to the northwest. However, most of the travel continued due west to Franklin Falls, where the route took them across the Saranac River on the way to Bloomingdale, where a fork in the road took them south to Saranac Lake, but if they continued straight they came to Paul Smiths. As it passed Noke's settlement and came toward Paul Smiths it followed the ridges of the hills. In Gabriels it crossed over Sanatorium hill and followed a course near the Downs property, then by way of Weller hill and McLaughlin's pasture to the present county road at the foot of Easy Street. Then up the hill toward Osgood Lake, following a course through what later was Paul Smith Hotel gardens and St. John's Cemetery, then crossed at the end of Church Pond over to the west side of Osgood close to the lake and on to McColloms, and on to Sam Meachem's place to the west of Meacham Lake where it turned northwest in the general direction of the east branch of the St. Regis River. Consider the time involved for such a trip when Franklin Falls was the mid-point and where the passengers and driver stopped for dinner.

As early as 1816 the State Legislature began to make an effort to get an improved road through our area in the form of the Northwest Bay Road which ran from

52

Lake Champlain (Westport) through Essex County to Franklin County and then across the towns of Harrietstown, Brighton, Duane, Santa Clara on to Hopkinton in St. Lawrence County.

In 1824 the legislature passed an act authorizing the commissioners to assess every free male inhabitant living on the road between Saranac River and Meacham Lake, not to exceed 10 days work each year. This was the method of improving roads in those days . . . a sort of tax payment in the shape of labor. However, it was not until 1898 that the State began to take steps in highway improvement in a real sense. Even then Franklin County was slow to take advantage of the expense sharing plan offered by the State.

Brighton did not wait for the county or the state to develop and improve their roads. In 1860 the Town Board voted to raise $250 in support of highways and bridges for the coming year. A. C. McCollom was the Highway Commissioner. This same amount was voted for several years and the Town divided its roads into five road districts. Inhabitants residing in each district were liable for, and assigned work on their own district road. In 1867 the amount was increased to $500 but dropped back to the original figure the following year. In 1872 the Board voted to build a new road from Barnum Pond to Burnt Ground (McCollom's).

The first mention of an overseer to be paid for opening roads in winter months came in 1875. Repercussions from a decision in 1877 not to plough or scrape roads after September first, came in the winter of 1879 when considerable discussion took place at the Board meeting in March about the terrible condition of the town roads from drifting snow and generally bad conditions that were impeding travel. Each road district was ordered to get busy and to give credit for road work on the taxed inhabitants.

In 1894 they bought stone and a stone crusher and put a stone surface on the road from Paul Smith's Hotel to the railroad station at Gabriels (then called Paul Smith's Station). While there had been a road through Rainbow, it was not authorized as a public highway until 1896. Over the years the support of the road program was mostly by labor contribution from the men who lived in an area rather than by taxation. Equipment was purchased by the Town, such as an iron road roller, a snow roller and road scraper, and a Michigan snow plow. By 1910 automobiles had invaded the country and the town was spending about $9,000 a year on roads and maintenance of them. It was in 1916 that they decided to cover the Gabriels to Paul Smith's road with asphalt . . . our first paved highway. Snow fencing was also introduced about this time in an effort to control drifting.

For several years after 1924 there was considerable negotiation over the elimination of the Butts railroad crossing on the Gabriels-Rainbow road where there had been several fatal accidents. It was finally eliminated with an overhead crossing. The crossing near Gabriels, also the scene of a fatal accident, was never removed.

Brighton was always considered to have the best roads in the area, probably because of the great influx of guests to the many hotels, which generated a definite feeling of need for improved roads. Even during depression times in the 1930's, road work went on. Macadam was put on the road from Riley's corner to Meagher's Mill in 1942.

While the curves and hills have been altered, the basic highway pattern of 1970 is the same as in the early days of the town. The highway coming into Brighton from Bloomingdale (Stage Route) met the road coming from Harrietstown about where it does now and they both proceeded through Gabriels toward Paul Smiths and from there north to McCollom's. The road from the Kesses

The stage coach at Paul Smiths, July 1884.

George Meserve, renowned stage driver.

Group of guides ready for a trip. Only two are known: Jim Cross, who was 6'6", seated on the cushion, and Orf Crary, seated No. 5.

Deer hunting party. Note the guide boat, deer hounds and deer.

Group picture taken in 1887 in front of the original house of Amos Rice, on the right, and the addition built by A. G. McCollom. Standing, left to right: David Hinkson, neighbor; unknown hunter; Clarence MacArthur with chain and dogs; unknown hunter; Orvie McNeil, neighbor; Ida Hinkson, neighbor; Mrs. Clarence MacArthur; Mrs. Amiel G. McCollom; Henry Merrill of North Lawrence; and Silas Merrill of Nicholville. Seated: Halcyon Hutchins, a sister of Mrs. MacArthur; and Amiel G. McCollom, holding Gladys MacArthur. (Photo courtesy of Maitland DeSormo)

Mr. DePeyster and his success. Fred Martin, guide with the dogs, and J. L. DePeyster, far right, are the only ones known.

Keese's Mill, August 1884.

Site of Keese's Mill Presbyterian Church. (Circa 1897)

Interior of a typical tent camp on St. Regis Lake in 1884.

A cabin constructed of logs, birch bark, and decorated with hunting mementos.

The unknown huntress was dressed for a fall outing with the dogs chained to her belt. A typical early camp on St. Regis.

The Rafferty Store in Gabriels, now the Leaning Pine Restaurant. (Photo courtesy Alice Warner)

The second Gabriels postoffice was located on the present main road near the entrance to the San.

J. Q. King meat wagon making a regular stop at Doty's Rainbow Cottage. Mrs. Orman Doty in the center, Carl Folson the driver. (Photo courtesy Doty family)

Frank Hobart in his potato fields near Gabriels.
(Photo courtesy Doty family)

The last Gabriels school, built in 1903.

Rainbow Lake School.

The last Easy Street School.

The Kesse's Mills School, original part on the right, addition on left.

St. John's in the Wilderness Church, 1877.

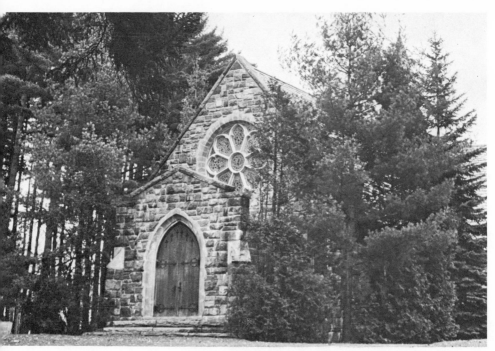

After the log church burned it was replaced in stone. St. John's in the Wilderness Episcopal Church as it is now.

Angel Gabriel Catholic Church at Paul Smiths.

Church of the Assumption Catholic Church at Gabriels.

Keese's Mills Presbyterian Church.

Gabriels Presbyterian Church.

Wardner's Rainbow Inn boathouse and garden.

First row (left to right): James M. Wardner, Addie Macomber Wardner, possibly Seth Wardner, Louise Wardner Prellwitz. The two children are sons of Louise, William and James Prellwitz. Second row: Mary Clark Wardner, Charles A. Wardner (parents of Walter Wardner), Katherine (Kit) Wardner Tack; next three are not known. (Photo courtesy of Walter Wardner)

Garondah Cottage at Rainbow Lake, early 1900's.

Camp Inglenook, built about 1905 at Clarke-Wardner's, Rainbow Lake.

*Group gathered for the dedication of St. Gabriel's Catholic
Church, Paul Smiths, August 16, 1894.*

Paul Smith's Hotel and Boathouse, north side. (Circa 1885)

Mills sawmill existed even before the Town of Brighton was formed.

The first automobile that penetrated the town arrived in July 1902. A honeymoon couple from Buffalo, Mr. and Mrs. Herbert Sacett, stopped for the night in Saranac Lake and came to Paul Smiths the next morning. The sensation it created along the way was long remembered, with animals and people alike frightened by the noise the machine made.

The railroad had crossed the northern part of the county in 1850 and had come up the Champlain Valley from the south a few years later. Sometime prior to 1858 the D. & H. had constructed a narrow gauge railroad to Ausable Forks. That was why Paul Smith had established a six-horse stagecoach to transport guests from there to his hotel, a distance of 50 miles, the horses being replaced with fresh teams at Franklin Falls. Some years later that distance was shortened when the D. & H. built their road through to Bloomingdale. But it was not until Dr. W. Seward Webb built the railroad that connected Malone with Utica by way of Tupper Lake, that the trains came through the Town of Brighton.

Construction on this road was started in 1891 and the first train to run came only as far as Saranac Lake on July 16, 1892. On October 24th that year the complete run to Utica took place. There were stops at Rainbow Lake, Gabriels (at first called Paul Smiths because of the hotel guests getting out there) and at Lake Clear Junction. Dr. Webb's road became a part of the New York Central a bit later and was in operation until the late 1950's.

Train service was excellent, especially during the 1920's and 30's when there were six trains a day. This service was very popular with the local people who wanted to shop in Malone or Saranac Lake. Local children traveled to and from school by the trains. Until the

55

automobile cut into their passenger business in the period following World War II, trains were the main mode of travel for the townspeople. Extra cars were put on at Malone Fair time each fall. Local resorts advertised that it was possible to make a trip to Montreal and back the same day and the railroad promoted Brighton resorts in their folders as early as 1894. Freights ran four to six trains a day, carrying all the goods that had to be shipped in and out of the area.

The tracks were removed from the town in 1961 and the right-of-way was purchased by the Niagara Mohawk Power Company and now carries high transmission lines of Seaway power to customers in the area.

In 1906 Paul Smith built a railroad on his own land over a distance of almost seven miles, from the New York Central Station at Lake Clear, to his hotel at Paul Smiths. This road made it possible for guests traveling from New York City to obtain Pullman reservations without having to make any changes along the way. Its first run was August 20, 1906. During 1906 and 1907 the train used steam power, but in July of 1908 Paul Smith electric power was used and this continued to be the power for the entire life of this train. The General Electric Company was responsible for the design of this special train and it was one of a kind in the history of railroading.

Guests could leave New York in the morning and have dinner at Paul Smiths' that evening, or they could leave in the evening and arrive for breakfast the following morning. Upon the morning arrival of a Pullman car the bellboy would serve hot coffee to its passengers or a complete breakfast to those who wanted it.

Many of the wealthy guests who came to Paul's hotel brought their own railroad cars and some pictures show several of these lined up on a siding awaiting the owner's desire to return home. Paul Smith's Electric Railroad continued to operate until 1932 when it was abandoned.

Chuckling in his own way, Paul told a newspaper reporter in September, 1911, that ... "The New York Central people laughed at me when they heard of my idea of my own railroad and said it couldn't be done . . . called it a paper railroad. But I started the men cutting the trees for the track line anyhow, and when it was done the Central folks wanted to buy it."

Exactly 10 years after the first automobile invaded the town, the second miracle of transportation swooped down on the area. On October 3, 1912, George Gray of Boston in a Burgess-Wright biplane sailed over the crest of Whiteface and landed at dusk in a wheat field near the Fletcher farm, near Bloomingdale. He had left Malone about an hour before and had made the trip at 6,000 feet. News of this arrival spread like wildfire and the following morning hundreds of automobiles converged on the spot. One of those who came was old Paul Smith who wanted to see this newest miracle of movement. In his lifetime he had arrived by oxen, had used horses for years, and was now in an automobile, and he urgently demanded a ride in this latest mode of locomotion. However, this was not to be, for the wind was so bad that his request was denied.

Aviation is now a regular part of our transportation plan. When the Paul Smith Power & Light Co. donated land for our present 1,200-acre Saranac Lake Airport in 1942, they established the area as a part of the air line system. The airport was dedicated July 10, 1949, and rededicated in 1973 with the installation of longer runways and the latest landing equipment suitable for jets. Over the years the port has been served by Eastern Airlines, Mohawk, Air North, and Allegheny Airlines on a regular basis and the Town of Brighton has been a contributing member of the Airport District organization since its inception.

Mail Service

The earliest Post Office to serve Brighton was at Bloomingdale. Once a week mail was brought by stage to those in the town. Those who were not directly on the stage route had some problems. For example, Wardner's at Rainbow built a mail box and placed it on the Military Road, and thus shortened the distance they had to go for mail. Sometimes they would drive out to try to meet the stage, but if this did not work, the driver of the stage would leave the mail in the box for Wardner to pick up later. In 1870 Smith's became a post office during the summer months, but during the winter they relied on sending a sleigh to Bloomingdale for the mail and newspapers.

According to the Post Office Department records it was March 17, 1881, when the first official Post Office was established at the Hotel with Apollos Smith as Postmaster. Paul remained in that capacity until his death. Old Paul used to brag about the fact that he could change his politics as fast as there was a change in the presidency for he always survived a political change. After his death, Paul, Jr., served from April 3, 1913, until Phelps took over May 15, 1927. Upon the death of Phelps, Richard J. Longtin was appointed and served until his retirement in 1958.

No permanent postmaster was appointed until 1961, but during this time William Hauptman and Margaret Monteau each served in acting capacity for about a year. It was decidedly a political football for a few years until

Joseph J. Farrell received his official appointment on April 24, 1961. He served until his death in November, 1968. William Fletcher then became acting postmaster. By this time the postmasterships were no longer a political appointment, but were secured from lists of eligible people who had passed appropriate examinations. Since Mr. Fletcher had passed this examination, he received his permanent appointment on May 15, 1971.

Early mail service was very poor and while stage delivery was reliable it was infrequent. It was a decided improvement when trains began to penetrate the north country. Lydia Martin Smith, Paul's wife, wrote in a letter dated 1/2/88, "The mail commenced running on the train from Saranac today." By the time the New York Central came through Gabriels and Rainbow, mail service reached its all time peak with six trains a day to bring in and take away the mail.

The next oldest Post Office in the town was established July 8, 1884, with James M. Wardner as Postmaster. It was first known as Rainbow, but the name was changed to Rainbow Lake on February 4, 1905. The location of the office here was dependent on who was Postmaster, and it has been in almost as many locations as there were Postmasters. From Wardner's Rainbow Inn to the Garondah, to the Brighton, to a spot near the school house, back down the road to the Rochester place, then to the Rainbow Sanitorium property; also in the little building next to Art Higgins' home, then up to Patnode's and back to one of the early sites in the present home of Postmaster Francis Hogan. The size of this office has varied but it presently serves a larger number of families than it ever did.

Postmasters of Rainbow

McColloms' was the third office established, September 16, 1897. Most of the time it was in the McCollom's Hotel but for about ten years (1924 on) Nettie Selkirk had it at the place we now know as Sunnyside Hotel. Postmasters who served it while it was an official office were:

This area is presently served by a rural carrier out of the Paul Smith office as is the Keeses Mill Road and Easy Street area.

When Barney Lantry sold the post office site to the Gabriels Sanatorium, he planned to resign so he must have been conducting the first office in Gabriels. This sale prompted the Sisters to negotiate to have the office left at the San as a majority of the patrons were in the San. So the earliest known office was on the San property and run by the Sisters. Mary O'Keefe received the appointment in 1898 and was followed by Sister Mary M. McCue in 1907. When Mary McCue died in November, 1934, a newspaper story stated that she was the only nun

Postmistress in the United States and that she had been appointed by President Teddy Roosevelt.

In 1898 there were only five boxholders at Gabriels: William Gandry, John Jenkins, E. J. King, George W. Porter, and G. V. Simmons. Mr. Gandry was a year-round boxholder so was considered the best customer. Ambrose Tebo, C. A. Davis, James P. Drury and Dr. Joseph Lamb signed up for boxes the following year. Other resident boxholders of Gabriels in the years that followed in the early 1900's were Maggy Ricketson, David Stern, Milly Stern, Fred Barnes, Joseph Alexander and his brother Frank, Ed Beany, Mrs. Charles Downs, Miss M. Fitzgerald, E. L. Green, Jute King, Arthur Leavitt (1902 on), Fred Martin (1901 on), David Russell, and George Paye.

Gabriels then was a fourth class postoffice and the pay was determined by the amount of money from total box rent collected and a commission on stamps cancelled. The total amount any postmaster could earn was $250 a quarter. Commission was based as follows:

on first $ 50.00 per quarter 100%
next $100.00 per quarter 60%
next $200.00 per quarter 50%
balance 40%

An example salary for Mary O'Keefe is worked as follows in the July-September quarter of 1898:

sold $99.87   earned $50.00
cancelled $92.08   earned $25.25

So, with box rents and money orders she earned a total of $99.97. During the October-December quarter that year she received $99.50, an indication of slightly better business in the summertime. Box rent was five and ten cents a quarter.

However, business was better in 1899, with eight call boxes sold, for the July quarter paid $159.63 and in 1900 it was up again with 14 call boxes sold and a total earned of $201.09.

By 1910 stamp sales were considerably increased as were the number of box holders and the same July quarter was paying nearly $300. Box rents were now 15c a quarter.

In the early 1950's this postoffice was listed as being third class and yearly salaries were close to the $4,000 mark.

Earl Martin became Postmaster in 1946 and served until his retirement in 1968, at which time his daughter, Rita Lancto, was appointed. In 1972 the Post Office was gutted by fire on a Sunday morning and in the investigation it was discovered that the safe had been "peeled" and robbed of stamps and cash. It was assumed that arson was the cause of the fire to cover up the theft. The office is now in a portable building on the Catholic Church parking lot.

Telephone - Telegraph

Originally the telegraph was brought in especially for the Paul Smith's Hotel and probably was used only in the summer at first. The exact date is not recorded, but it was there in 1874 when Trudeau spent the winter with the Smith family. This much is known, for Trudeau told in his autobiography of learning the Morse code so that he could hold conversations with the operator in Plattsburgh during the evenings. This not only gave him something to hold his interest while he was recuperating from a severe bout with tuberculosis, but it also gave them all an opportunity to keep up on all the news of the country.

Over the years this service was expanded as the hotel grew and the entire community was able to benefit from the opportunity to send and receive messages this way.

In the years before the telephone became so universal, the telegraph was a very important means of communication and was used extensively. Western Union finally withdrew its machine from Paul Smiths sometime in the 1950's and just maintained the Saranac Lake office for those who wanted to use the service. By this time the telegraph was no longer the major means of communication.

A telephone company formed by F. M. Bull, a Saranac Lake druggist, for the purpose of affording communications between the numerous business centers and summer resorts in the area, began to serve Wardner's Rainbow Inn in 1884. Mr. Bull had his men string the lines and install the instruments while Wardner had his men cut the cedar poles and set them in place.

It was hard to understand what was said over the phones and much confusion resulted. Some of this confusion was amusing, such as the time Phil King listened over the wire. He was on the phone during a thunderstorm when a loud report came from the sky. He was supposed to be talking to his wife, Jane, when the thunder came, and he said, "Yep, that's Jane all right" as he dropped the receiver, convinced at last that the phone was working and that it really was her.

A simple hook-up between buildings was another early telephone system in Brighton. Some handy workman at the Paul Smith's Hotel rigged it up and that was the beginning of the telephone system that was expanded to serve the entire area a bit later.

On March 29, 1900, the Brighton Town Board granted the exclusive right and franchise, to erect, construct and forever maintain a telegraph and telephone system within the town. By 1915 there were 100 phones in use.

The first phones were battery-operated and were mounted on the wall. Several homes shared a common line with different rings for each party. When the phone rang for one party, every one else on the line knew there was a call and for whom the call was. It can be safely assumed that the party line was a source of much eaves-dropping. In fact, to use the phone you had to lift the receiver in order to determine whether someone else was using it, before you could crank up enough of a ring to rouse the operator on the switchboard, and thus place your call. If you wanted to converse with someone on your own line you could just crank out the number of rings yourself and get your party. The operator was also an easy means of locating the whereabouts of someone you might be looking for but could not locate easily. For example, the operator might be likely to know where the doctor might be found, or could summon help in any type of emergency.

The switchboard at Paul Smith's was located for years in the Hotel and was relocated in the Smith Cottage after the big hotel burned in 1930. In the Smith Cottage (enlarged into a hotel) the switchboard, Post Office and telegraph were all located in the same two-room area on the first floor near the entrance. The same men who worked in the Post Office were also the operators of the other two facilities. Sometimes it was a pretty hectic place, especially in the later years after World War II when phones became more numerous, and in almost constant use by some customers. Most of the party lines, by this time, had more than eight parties on a line and the competition to get a line was pretty keen. There was no such thing as a private line. The other problem was that all long-distance calls had to go through Saranac Lake and there were only three long distance trunks available. The board by this time was overworked and out-of-date. Everytime something went wrong with the equipment, it was difficult, if not impossible, to get it repaired. Toward

64

the end, there was only one man who had experience enough on this old set-up to be able to repair it, if he could get the parts.

Unbelievable as it may seem today, there were times of the day when there were no operators on the board, and sometimes during the night the operator might fall asleep during a quiet time. If this happened it would be quite a while before the insistant ringing would rouse him from his nap. As late as 1946, the lunch period from twelve to two on Sunday was a bad time to put a call through. This was the time when the operator would plug in the Gabriels San to a long distance line and go to the dining room to have his dinner in peace.

After the College began in 1946 business increased so much for the phone company that a full time operator was hired and service improved in some ways. Sometime in the late fifties when a new phone was required, the wall-type were replaced with an instrument that sat on the table, but you still had to crank it to ring the operator. Some improvement was reached on the campus lines, however, for these phones installed were such that you could just raise the receiver to get the operator.

When the Smith Cottage hotel burned in 1962, the old switchboard was destroyed and many problems had to be faced in trying to re-estsablish phone service because of the out-of-date equipment in the company. It was not long after this that the College, as owner of the Company, sold the telephone franchise to the AuSable Telephone Company of Keeseville, New York.

When the new owners took over there were many months of preparations needed before the customers noticed any appreciable change. A new building was erected on the Paul Smith road across from the Episcopal Church to house the new equipment. All the lines (cables) were placed underground or under water. All lines were private and the toll-free area was extended to include Saranac Lake. Previous to that, any call to Saranac Lake was a toll call. The new phones themselves were in a wide assortment of colors and they were push button dial type. Direct dialing to any place in the country was now available to Town of Brighton homes.

All this was installed and made ready and tested befor being put into use on December 21. 1969. On this date the next to the last manual phone system in the state went out of use. The *Essex County Republican* in an 1884 issue reported that a telephone line was being built between the Paul Smith's Hotel and Bloomingdale. This fact pretty well established that the system was one of the earliest in the country.

Electric Power

Electric power first came to Brighton in 1898 when Paul Smith converted a water-power sawmill that had been a part of the operation of Pat Ducey at the outlet of Lower St. Regis Lake, known as Keeses Mills, into a 150 KW hydroelectric generating plant. He then built power lines into the hotel grounds and buildings to supply 3,000 incandescent lights inside and 200 arc lights outside on the grounds.

The Brighton Town Board minutes recorded that on March 29, 1900, the Paul Smith Hotel Co. was granted the exclusive rights to erect, construct and forever maintain an electric system in the Town, as well as a telegraphy and telephone system. Paul was looking ahead to the time when he would have more power and it was soon after this that he began a series of business moves that led to the formation of the Paul Smith Electric Light & Power Co.

In 1903, Paul purchased a water-power site at Franklin Falls on the Saranac River opposite the hotel where he was married. That same year he also bought another site at Union Falls, seven miles downstream. Through his Hotel Company he purchased all the lands that were to be flooded through the construction of a dam at both of these sites. The Power Company, when formed in 1905, had Paul Smith as President and immediately began building transmission lines from these power plants to Bloomingdale and thence to Paul Smiths. Later, lines were extended to Saranac Lake and other local areas.

There is an interesting insight revealed in the following story about Paul. P. B. McKay was the man hired as a contractor to take care of developing the power sites along with Lem Merrill, the well-known surveyor from Loon Lake, as the civil engineer. Before Paul closed the deal, the boys, Paul, Jr., and Phelps, feeling sure that their father had made a poor calculation of the possibilities, sent a request to P. T. Hanscom to come up in a hurry to advise them. Mr. Hanscom, then with General Electric, had become a fast friend of the family after he originally came to help set up the Keeses Mills installation. His study of the suitability of the water at Franklin Falls and Union indicated that Paul's decision to buy was not only wise but farsighted as well. So this reassured the boys and they quit trying to block their father in his deal.

Construction on the two power projects was started in the winter of 1904-05 and the work on Union was completed in 1907. That same year he bought Saranac Lake Light, Heat and Power Co., which included the generating station in the village. This particular site was in constant use, 24 hours a day, until World War II when,

67

according to a workman's statement, the generators and water-wheels were sold for scrap as an aid to the war effort. Work on the Franklin Falls plant was not completed until 1911.

The controversy with the State of New York that arose in 1905 began with the start of work on the two dam sites and lasted for seven years. While the final decision was a victory for Paul over the State it is safe to say that the decision of the judge would be highly questionable by today's standards. According to accounts of the legal battling in the New York State Forest, Fish & Game Reports, the State claimed that the Power Company deliberately filled its reservoirs at Franklin Falls and in so doing backed the river up, flooding a considerable quantity of state-owned timberland, causing injury and destruction of this timber. Of course, this was a violation of State regulations that forbade flooding any State land for any reason. The Power Company had been denied their petition to build the dams, but had proceeded anyhow. What with restraining injunctions by the State and delaying motions by the Company, the whole thing dragged on until the work was completed and so, like the final judgement, was the only way to decide the case as long as the deed was done.

After Paul's death in 1912, his son Phelps took over the office of president and, shortly after this, power was contracted to Lake Placid and in 1925 Tupper Lake began to buy power from the Company.

It was in 1925 when Paul, Jr., in failing health, gave Phelps the controlling share of the Company and sold the balance to Associated Gas & Electric. This left Phelps the only member of the family remaining in the Company but he held the controlling interest. It was under Phelps' management that the three-story office building in Saranac Lake was built in 1927 over an old flume on the same site as the generating station. This is the same building used by Niagara Mohawk for their local office at the present time.

After the death of Phelps in 1937, a long-time employee of the Company, Richard J. Longtin, became the president. Mr. Longtin, who had come as a young man in 1908 to work for the Smiths, had been active in the entire development period and it was logical that he should be the one to take over the leadership of the company. He was responsible for the construction of the new dam in Saranac Lake and the improvement of the shores around Lake Flower and the Company contributed to the development of Riverside Park. By this time, company facilities had begun to age and Mr. Longtin initiated a rebuilding program. By 1938 the increased use of power made it impossible to meet the demand and it became necessary to purchase additional power from New York State Gas & Electric. The Piercefield Diesel Plant was added in 1949, and further enlarged in 1953. The famous "blowdown" of November 1950 did enormous damage to the lines and other equipment and it was several days before power was able to be restored to normal operation. By the time Mr. Longtin retired in 1963 because of poor health, the company had rebuilt 85% of the system. Dr. Chester L. Buxton, President of the College, which owned the Company after Phelps' will created the College, became President of the Power Company.

By the summer of 1965 the Company was buying over half of its electricity for distribution and further trouble occurred when the rusted surge tank at Union fell to the ground, eliminating its further use. Beset by many problems, it was decided to complete the negotiations, already started, with the sale of Paul Smith Company to Niagara Mohawk Power Company in the fall of that same year.

Niagara Mohawk, the present electric utility serving

the town, receives Seaway power for its customers by means of the new high line system constructed on the old New York Central Railroad right-of-way which they purchased after the railroad was abandoned.

Education

Formal education in the early days of the town was pretty scarce. In 1855 there were no schools in the entire area from Saranac Lake to Duane. Settlers, that could, taught their own children to read and write but for the majority it was a case of the children growing up illiterate.

Lydia Martin Smith was well educated and taught her boys, Henry, Phelps and Paulie, at home. Some of the other children came for lessons once in a while, but not on a regular basis.

Soon it was realized that a school was badly needed and the first one was started in 1867 at Keeses Mills, for this was the area where the greatest concentration of families was located. Ann Goodspeed came from St. Armand, as the first teacher to open the school of three students on November 18, 1867, according to the attendance records. This session ran until February 21, 1868, when it must be assumed that weather and roads became too bad. When it reopened on May 4th there were 16 children in attendance and they went to classes until August 7th. Melifa Goodspeed and Hattie Clark were also early teachers here. In 1892 Anna M. Scanlin received $128 for the fall term of 16 weeks and the children totaled 28 in attendance.

The number of children continued to increase at

Keeses Mills so that by early 1900's it was evident that a larger school was required. As you face the school, the section to the right was the original part and the addition is to the left. The new part was completed in 1911. From then on two teachers were needed.

The school districts were completely defined in 1870 when the second school in the town was built in the Gabriels area. It was a one-room log building located between the Rand place (Split Rock) and the road that came to Rainbow. It was furnished with double seats and desks and had blackboards made by painting a wide black strip on the plastered walls. Windows were placed high enough so the children could not be distracted by what they might see outside. This burned at an early date and when it was replaced it was located on the site of the present one. This was also a one-room school. Later when the district decided to have a larger building, Fred Martin bought it and moved it across the road. After some additional construction, it is now the Charles Martin house. Charles is the son of Fred Martin.

The new two-room school in Gabriels was built in 1901, and these are the two rooms on the front of the present building. The back rooms were added at a later date. The taxpayers of District No. 4 can be justifiably proud of this structure for it was maintained over the years with much care and thought.

The Easy Street area was also developing as a residential section and the third school of the town was built here in 1871. The original school was built just beyond the top of Easy Street Hill on the left side of the road. On one side of the school was a burying ground and on the other side the Methodist Church was built a bit later. It was a one room building heated by a box stove. The opening term was presided over by Melifsa Goodspeed and it ran from November 20, 1871, to February 23, 1872, with 14 children in attendance. The Smith boys are reported to have attended classes here and the story goes that they drove a dog team to get to school.

About 1900 another school was built about mid-way up the hill across from the Quarters home to replace the first building. On May 7, 1947, after a particularly heated annual school meeting this school burned to the ground. The fire was discovered by a neighbor who tried to save some things but the flames were too for advanced. The taxpayers of District No. 1 met to discuss the situation and it was decided to build a replacement as soon as possible. An attractive modern wooden building consisting of one large main room was completed in 1948, but until it was ready to use the children attended classes in the Town Hall at the foot of Easy Street.

The Rainbow children attended classes in one of the Wardner farm buildings for a while in a sort of branch school that was considered a part of Gabriels. Also some of the time they were transported to Gabriels by wagon or sleigh. Later a small one-room building was built about a mile beyond Wardner's on the road to Gabriels, on the right hand side. This is presently being used as a home after some remodeling by the owner, Mary Recore.

James Wardner was School Commissioner for District No. 4 of Franklin County for six years beginning in 1882. It was his job to visit every school in his district twice a year, and to conduct teacher's examinations for certification. He also had to conduct a yearly teachers' institute. The Town of Brighton was included in his District.

By 1890 there were four school districts in the town—No. 1 was Easy Street, No. 2 Keeses Mills, No. 3 McColloms, and No. 4 Gabriels, with its branch at Rainbow Lake. This was from Commissioner Wardner's report of that year. Seven teachers were employed, one male and six female. There were 110 children attending school. The value of the buildings was considered to be $2,475.

72

Public money from the State came to $548.39 while the local taxpayers raised $820.80 with the assessed valuation of the district placed at $131,895. Mr. Wardner reported that there had been a big improvement in the school buildings. He regretted that stormy weather and impassable roads had forced him to make fewer official visits, but he had made eight. (This was considerably more than Commissioner M. E. McClary made in 1892 ... he made only two.) Commissioner Wardner said that the same poor conditions had contributed largely to the decline of pupil attendance. He stated that in some sections students had long walks through sparsely settled areas and that also took its toll on the attendance report.

In the spring of 1929 at a special meeting of the taxpayers and the board it was decided to organize a Junior High department. The Grange Hall property of Charles Tebo was remodeled, painted, and equipped for the 26 students who enrolled. This new program was modeled after the plan of the Saranac Lake school. When it opened September 17, 1929, mathematics, Latin, French, English and history were among the subjects offered.

School attendance records give testimony to the various epidemics that swept the town. Scarlet fever was active in January of 1902 and the Gabriels school was closed for two weeks. Easy Street was also closed in February, 1912, for the same reason when the Alexanders and the Watson Swinyer families were struck down. In 1917 and 1918 Gabriels had another outbreak of scarlet fever and chickenpox during February. Diphtheria visited Easy Street in October, 1917.

The year 1917 brought the first physical education program to Brighton school districts and their share of the cost was placed at $400. Esther Hubbell was listed as the teacher for this program.

Truant officers were expected to visit each district school once a month or oftener if called by the teacher.

Their job was to make sure that children attended school regularly. The first mention of an appointment to this position in town records was in 1910 when Ambrose Tebo was named to the post. Hardy Paye, Henry Hobart, George Riley, Claude Sweet, and Louis Strack served in that order. Originally the pay for calls to the schools was based on the following scale:

District No. 1—$2.00 per day   District No. 3—$4.00 per day
District No. 2—$3.00 per day   District No. 4—$1.00 per day

By 1923 Louis Strack was on a flat rate of $17.00 per month, and this continued into the 1930's when no further mention was made of this position in Town Board records.

The first mention of a teacher with a Normal School education was in 1902. Regents examinations were first noted in 1914. Salaries were quoted on a monthly basis of $56 each month and in 1900 school was being conducted on a September to June program as we know it. By the 1920's teachers were being paid about $1,000 to $1,200 a school year.

In the late 1950's pressure from the State Education Department was being put on the various districts to join with Saranac Lake in a centralization program. For many years the districts had been sending all high school students to the Saranac Lake High School, bussing the students to and from Saranac Lake each day. The cost of transportation plus tuition for each student was a part of the budget for each school district, paid for by the taxpayers. The State's position was that a better, less costly education could be available to all students if a larger unit was formed, in a centralized program. This area was one of the last in the State to comply when they finally voted to form the Saranac Lake Central School District in July, 1964. This meant that the individual schools would gradually be closed and all children, kindergarten through high school, would be bussed to designated central schools. For a time the Gabriels and Easy Street schools were used but they were closed in the late '60's and by 1970 none of the schools built by the Town of Brighton were in use. Easy Street and Rainbow schools have been sold to individuals.

The earliest education was kept to the basics. It was probably meager, judging by present-day standards. Learning to read was the most important job of the scholars, and next came the mastery of simple arithmetic. Sometimes a particular teacher was able to arouse special interests in singing or drawing, but it was the exception rather than the rule. However, these early schools did bring the children together and provided a meeting place where they were bound to experience some social activities and learning experiences not to be duplicated in the home. This form of learning took place while eating their lunches brought from home, as well as on the playground before and after classes.

In the back of the yearly attendance record for 1875 there was a questionnaire that the teacher was supposed to complete. To the series of questions, teacher Maggie Ricketson answered in the following way:

What educational magazine did you read? ....“None”
Have you ever attended teachers institute? ....“Never”
When and where did you last attend a .... “I tell you I never did and
  meeting of said association?   whatsmore, I never will.”

There was a space in this yearly record for a list of the visitors and in 1917 one of the visitors to Keeses Mills School was Leonard Houghton (faculty member at Paul Smiths' College later). Several years ago Leonard told me that, as a young man, he toured on his bicycle to visit schools and conducted a sort of physical training class. Interesting to note that he returned to the area as a college teacher.

Sometimes there was some reference to the facilities

75

of the school . . . like one year, "two good privies" were listed. You can be sure that these were of the outdoor variety, in a separate building.

"A COLLEGE FOR FRANKLIN COUNTY" ran as newspaper headlines when the will of Phelps Smith was filed for probate in 1937, shortly after his death. After some specific gifts, his will directed as follows: "I give, devise and bequeath the remainder of my estate for the erection and maintenance of a college of higher education for boys and girls to be known as Paul Smith's College of Arts and Sciences." The estate was estimated at over seven million, largely real estate, and from the date of the will, February 21, 1928, the project was one long planned by Phelps as a memorial to his father . . . Paul Smith, the pioneer hotelman of the Adirondacks.

The Regents of the University of the State of New York recorded the charter October 15, 1937, with the following people directed to organize the college: John R. Freer, John M. Cantwell, Jr., Hilda Fletcher, O. Byron Brewster, Thomas F. Conway, Mrs. J. Gales Holcombe, Horace H. Lamberton, Lithgow Osborne, Earl MacArthur, and John B. Trevor.

There were many delays and difficulties facing the paper college . . . delays created by disappointed Smith relatives; disagreements among the incorporating trustees, and the onset of World War II. The original intent of Phelps Smith was to have an institution of higher education with buildings, faculty and students located in the Town of Brighton, but there were those who preferred to interpret his desires by the giving of scholarships to young people to attend other colleges. In a long board meeting that was marked by sharp debate, a close eight to seven vote defeated the plan to have a junior college set up immediately. However, this intense debate did create a compromise plan, in which the scholarships would be given for the present, but a president would be

76

hired at once. His first duty was to study the problems of establishing a college at Paul Smiths, taking into consideration the terms of the will, requirements of the Charter, and the Board of Regents, as well as the physical and financial means available.

The man selected for this difficult job of planning a collegiate establishment to satisfy the various interests involved was Earl C. MacArthur, chosen from the original incoporating Trustees. He was a local son, born at McColloms on July 15, 1888, and received his early education there and in Malone. He was graduated from Yale in 1910 and for nearly thirty years taught English at Peddie Institute in New Jersey. President MacArthur served the College from 1937 until December, 1945. It was during this time that the many litigations and other difficulties as well as World War II prevented the College from opening. The campus was used for training a WAC contingent, as a base for Signal Corp. training, and as a summer school.

The Signal Corp. operation at the College began July 13, 1942, with a class of about 60 men and a faculty of six. Over a period of a year, more than 400 were trained in radio technology for the Army. An auxiliary program for women was begun in early June, 1943, but by September the government decided to take only those women who would enlist in the Army directly. By September the entire Army operation at Paul Smiths was closed down because of the ample supply of radio technicians.

The buildings that had been used in the C.C.C. program were given to the College in March, 1943. These were close by in the Osgood-Barnum Pond area and at one time were considered useful for the housing of students. However, with the cessation of the Signal Corp. training program they were not needed as the immediate campus facilities left over from hotel days were sufficient.

The next school operation of the College came during

the summer of 1944 when a special program of intensive study was offered. This program made it possible for a student to select a single subject which was studied with at least three hours of classroom instruction daily for two weeks. The next two weeks another subject could be studied. The idea was to give someone who had only two weeks' vacation an opportunity to participate. A total of 23 intensive courses were taken by the different groups of the 260 students who enrolled. The students who came were composed of teachers, college students and business executives, with more of the latter group attending. The faculty was outstanding, coming from top men in industry and well-known educational institutions. This was considered an unqualified success, but it was not repeated.

When President MacArthur resigned in December, 1945, over serious philosophical differences with the Trustees, the college was without a leader for a short time.

The second President of Paul Smith's College, named in spring of 1946, was Frederick G. Leasure, a native of Kansas, who had received his M.A. at Columbia and had done advanced graduate work at George Washington University. He came with wide experience in directing Agricultural Institutes, both in the United States and abroad. The Board of Trustees authorized the expenditure of $250,000 for modernization and winterizing the former hotel and resort buildings so that they might be used by the college as plans went ahead for the opening in September, 1946. Early announcements reaffirmed that the new college would be co-educational, and that dormitory, shop and classroom space would be available for 150 students. President Leasure soon had scores of workmen busy at painting, insulating, wiring, and rebuilding the former resort facilities. Many a crisis marked the slightly more than two years that Mr. Leasure served as President of the College, but the actual operation did get under way. The response of students was most encouraging, with about 250 students enrolled by the second year. There were many local students and about 80% were veterans, just out of service from World War II. Three programs of study were offered from the first year: Liberal Arts, Forestry, and Hotel Management. At first the Arts program was most popular but soon the steady growth of the other two offerings far exceeded the growth of the Arts registration.

President Leasure stayed only two years, resigning when disagreements with the Board of Trustees could not be resolved. A new president was selected before Mr. Leasure left the campus in June, 1948, so there was no interruption in the College programs.

Chester L. Buxton of the Clarkson College faculty assumed his position as the third President of Paul Smith's College on July 1, 1948. Mr. Buxton was from Ohio and did his college work at Mount Union College, Case Institute, and Western Reserve University. He had been a teacher for several years in Cleveland high schools and had served on the Clarkson faculty for nine years before becoming director of the Malone branch of Clarkson in 1946. Not all the growing pains were over for the little college, but the new director applied his own brand of leadership and so became the first president to weather the difficulties that beset the new venture.

After the first few years the number of veterans attending declined and so the enrollment was reduced. A program of recruitment was instituted at the high school level and gradually as the College became better known the registration began climbing again. Presently about 1,200 students are registered with the greatest number in the forestry program. While the college is co-educational, there has always been an overwhelming majority of men in the student body regardless of the attempts to encourage girls to come.

While some of the original buildings, like the store and several cottage residences, are still in use, most have disappeared from the campus, either by fire or demolition. Ten new dormitories have been constructed, several classroom facilities, a library, a gymnasium, an administration building, and several faculty residences have been built. In addition to the construction on the campus, a gift of the White Pine Camp property, the purchase of the Hotel Saranac in Saranac Lake and the Gabriels Sanitorium property in Gabriels has further added to the already large campus. Both students and faculty use White Pine on Osgood for housing and classrooms in the forestry program. This is also true of the Gabriels Sanitorium property.

As of 1975, Dr. Buxton is still President of the College that uses about 155 full-time employees of which about 70 make up the faculty and staff. The annual budget totals about $2,500,000, half of which goes for wages and salaries.

Over five thousand young men and women have been graduated in the following departments, as of June, 1975:

Forestry 2,960
Hotel Management and Business Administration.... 1,637
Liberal Arts 719
Ecology and Environmental Technology 16*

*While Associate degrees have been granted since the early 1950's, this was the first year when degrees were awarded for this program.

Churches

Although various ministers held services in the parlor at Paul Smith's Hotel during the summer months for the guests and guides, there was no official church in Brighton until the late 1870's. Dr. Edward Livingston Trudeau, a year-round guest at that time, and his wife had been conducting a Sunday School for the children in the nearby school house. They sparked considerable interest among other guests in the fall of 1876 to start a drive for funds to build a church. Dr. Trudeau interested Mrs. Louis Livingston in the project and she raised $1,400 by holding a fair in her parlors in New York City. Other guests responded to the appeal, and Paul Smith contributed the logs and the land.

The little log chapel was designed by a New York architect, a Mr. Hawthorne, who gave his services to the cause. The finest white pine logs, oiled to perfection, were used for the exterior. The roof was shingled. The almost square building, with the chancel at the north end, had interior walls of stone colored plaster, and wainscoted with black walnut. The ceiling was arched and tinted blue. All the furnishings, including the organ, were donated and Dr. Trudeau had carefully supervised the construction. The total cost was between three and four thousand dollars. The chapel was all completed and free of debt when Bishop William C. Doane of Albany consecrated St. John's in the Wilderness Church of Paul Smiths on September 13, 1877. It had been deeded to the Board of Missions of the Episcopal Church.

At first, services were held only when there was a clergyman guest at the hotel or when one was nearby, but later Rev. C. S. Knapp, an invalid, was put in charge during the summer months, which was the only time that services were held regularly. The original seating capacity was only about 40 and this soon became too small. So another appeal for funds was started and J. Lawrence Aspinwall, a cousin of Dr. Trudeau, began the delicate job of transformation. The nave, at the north end, was left untouched; a transept was added on each side and the chancel was enlarged so that it became cruciform shape, seating 150 people easily. This was done in 1893, and the end result was a simple, beautiful place of worship enhanced by stained glass windows with oiled black ash pews and furniture.

Margaret Cranford, whose family has camped on Osgood since 1889, remembers going to St. John's with her grandparents. She was quite a small child at the time and she recalls the mortar and moss used to fill the cracks between the logs.

This lovely log church was totally destroyed by fire in the early hours of Sunday morning, December 4, 1928. The present stone church was erected in replacement. Miss Cranford recalls that after the fire Dr. Trudeau started a campaign right away for a new church. He requested the campers to contribute stone for a new one. People could buy one stone or as many as they chose and each would be cut. There were stones in memory of her grandparents, and many others who had been there and loved the place made similar contributions. The present church, seating about 150, was designed by architect William Diston and his associate, Arthur G. Wilson, of Saranac Lake.

The new stone church has a slate roof and it is a beautiful building with its stained glass windows. One is a rose window, a gift of the Ogden Reid family, that includes one of their famous sail boats. In August, 1947, two more stained glass windows were given by Mrs. Clarkson Runyon, a summer resident of Upper St. Regis Lake.

The congregation voted to change the status of the church from a mission to that of an incorporated parish in 1951, with Dr. F. B. Trudeau as the Senior Warden and Mrs. R. S. Rauch the Junior Warden.

From 1966-1970 church was held each week on a year round basis, for the College was fortunate to have an Episcopalian minister on its faculty. Rev. George Easter, who for many years had been a camper on the lakes, was the regular minister while he was at the College.

According to James Wardner's journal, for many years arrangements were made with the Methodist minister in Bloomingdale to hold services in the Brighton school house on Sunday afternoons. A church society was formed to help pay the minister's salary. They also hoped to build a church because the school was too small and the seats too narrow for adults.

Phil King used to invite everyone to his big farm home to an oyster supper to raise money for the minister. In the evening after the supper there would be games and entertainment.

Methodist Church records of Saranac Lake show in a report that D. W. Harris "labored fruitfully" in Brighton, near Keeses Mills, during 1861 and '62, going every two weeks to preach. No mention was made of where the services were held. In 1871, records indicate that a circuit rider preacher made his rounds on horseback every two weeks, coming from Bloomingdale to conduct his service.

Although you would not recognize it today as being a church, the house where William Stalker and William Rutherford lived was originally a Methodist Church when it was built in 1893. The money for building this church was raised by Mrs. Paul Smith, although she was a Presbyterian. A resident clergyman from Bloomingdale conducted services there every other Sunday. Folks recall that in back of the church was a long shed with stalls and people arriving drove their horses to the back, tying the horses so they could feed but leaving the wagon attached. No one remembers just when they stopped having services here but as near as can be determined they stopped about 1920. Then it was made over into a residence by a man by the name of Ackerman. It is presently owned by the College and used as a faculty residence.

The first Roman Catholic Church in Brighton was that of the Angel Gabriel at Paul Smiths, organized in 1894 by the Rev. Ferdinand J. Lussier, who was then pastor of the church at Brandon. It was located about a quarter of a mile from Paul Smiths Hotel on land donated by Paul. The church was built soon after this and was blessed by Rev. Michael Holland in 1896. It is a simple wooden building with a seating capacity of about one hundred. This church, with some modernization, is still in use.

While it is not known who served the church in the very first years, the following have served since 1907, according to Gladys Blanchard's notes.

Nov. 1907-April 1927 . . . . Father Joseph Berard
April 1927-March 1950 . . . . Father Edgar A. Gallagher
March 1950-May 1950 . . . . Father Page
June 1950-Nov. 1955 . . . . Father John Richardson
Nov. 1955-July 12, 1961 . . . . Father Joseph E. Dowd
July 12, 1961-June 14, 1969 . . . . Father Paul LaRock
June 14, 1969-March 10, 1971 . . . . Father John Pendergast
March 10, 1971-   . . . . Father Robert O. Lamatie

The early settlers of Catholic faith in Rainbow Lake and Gabriels attended religious services in the Chapel of the Sanitorium Gabriels, which was started in 1896. Services were also held for a time in a large hall over Riley's apartment house. Father O'Donnell came from

Alder Brook to conduct these services. Later Father Jean Lucien served the Sanitorium.

In the latter teens Fathers Burke and Murtaugh, patients at the Sanatorium Gabriels, realized that a church was greatly needed in Gabriels. They started a fund drive which made it possible to erect the Church of the Assumption which is presently in use at Gabriels. Under the supervision of Father Dumont, a newly appointed pastor, work was begun in 1922 on the field stone and stucco building that is situated in the center of Gabriels. When the building was completed in 1923 the seating capacity was about 200. Services have been conducted on a year-round basis ever since.

Ill health forced the retirement in 1936 of Father Dumont and he was succeeded by Father Donald Gallagher, who left in March, 1944, to go into the U.S. Armed Forces. A Father Thompson came for a few years to be followed by Father Francis McMahon, who served more than twenty years. Presently, Father Albert Plante is the priest.

The Presbyterian Church built at Keeses Mills came about when Rev. William B. Lusk was graduated from Princeton Seminary in 1897 and was appointed Superintendent of the Adirondack Mission that included several little churches in this northern area of New York State. Through the influence of some college friends, he finally settled at Paul Smiths to live while looking after all his churches. After he came in the spring of 1897 he conducted services every Sunday in the Keeses Mills school. Quite a number of people around the area attended these services. The adults mostly preferred to stand around the wall as the school seats were too small for them. This and other factors influenced Rev. Lusk to attempt to build a church.

He appealed to Paul Smith for the land and the site he chose was the knoll overlooking the old mill dam on the St. Regis River where that first sawmill had been located by Keese and Tomlinson. Mrs. Anson Phelps Stokes, the Penfolds, Whitelaw Reid, Henry Hotchkiss, and others contributed time and money to get the church built. William L. Coulter of Saranac Lake was engaged to design the building and soon, with the cooperation of the people of the community, the church was ready for dedication on July 15, 1899.

Mrs. Stokes' son, the Rev. A. P. Stokes, who had just completed his course and was an Episcopalian minister, was the special speaker invited for the occasion.

Rev. Lusk invited Paul Smith to come to the dedication as a special guest. Since Paul was not a regular church goer, Rev. Lusk peeped down once in a while to Paul's pew to see how he was behaving. Paul seemed to be very much at ease, except every time St. Paul was mentioned, he appeared to be a little embarrassed, as if the allusion were to himself. At the close of the service, the two ministers went around greeting the people. As they came up to Paul, Rev. Lusk said to him: "Now that you have started to come to church, Uncle Paul, why don't you keep it up and come next Sunday?"

The reply came promptly: "No, Reverend, the last sermon I heard did me twenty years," and then, looking at Rev. Stokes with a merry twinkle in his eyes, he added: "This was a much better one. It will do me the rest of my life."

George Skiff was the first sexton of the church and Rev. Lusk served as minister until 1906. He recalls that the little church was filled from the first with rich and poor alike and he felt that the chief reason was the friendly feeling that prevailed, so everyone felt perfectly at home. While he directed his preaching to the parents, he concentrated much of his effort on the children. At each service he would have about 20 of the young folks form a semi-circle in the front of the church and recite verses from the Bible. Among the children who gathered around Rev. Lusk were Hardy Sweet, Gordon Tyler, Raldy Martin, Bessie and Sylvia Newell, Harold Newell, Maude Crary, Sarah Hyde, Beulah, Cora, Carrie and Jim Sawyer. He personally paid them five cents a verse, not exactly the proper method, he admitted, but one which insured the introduction of the Bible to each and every home.

Those who lived near the church did not have too many problems in getting there. However, those who lived some distance and the campers on the lakes had quite a hard time. Since most everyone had a boat of some sort in those days, it was decided to construct a boat landing at an arm of Upper St. Regis River just a mile from the church and cut a trail over the little ridge that brought people almost to the church door. When this was completed it made a pleasant walk for those who came by boat from the Upper and Lower Lakes. Theodore Roosevelt's sister Anna, who was the wife of Admiral William S. Cowles, and her cousin, Helen Roosevelt, were regular in their attendance during the summer months.

During the succeeding years countless prominent campers, who spent their summers in the area, continued to lend support to this church. In the early 1900's the old Skiff homestead, across the road from the church, was bought and remodeled for a clubhouse where, during the winter months, the guides and their families met for recreation and fellowship. A pool table was secured, and while Mr. Anderson was minister, the men would often gather for a round or so of boxing. Sunday school met there and the ladies of the church held their famous "suppers" there as a part of their constant efforts to raise money for the church. This was the location of the annual summer bazaar where they sold many hand-made articles to the summer people and visitors who were anxious to help the church and at the same time pick up little gifts for future giving.

As the church grew, it became apparent about 1960 that the clubhouse was too small so plans were made to build a larger one on the water close by the church. This was built by the members themselves, who came in their spare time to work, over a period of several years, completing it in 1965. Suppers and Sunday school continue to keep this new building a busy place. The church also owns a house close by, for the minister to live in.

The 50th anniversary was celebrated with a special service on Sunday, July 17, 1949, with Rev. Lusk again giving the sermon like in the old days. So many came that there was nowhere near enough room inside. After the service there was a family picnic for all and old friends gathered in groups to eat their lunch. The celebration continued all the following week with the church bazaar, and concluded with a square dance at Paul Smith's College gym on Friday night.

Another celebration of the building of the church came along with the 60th anniversary on July 19, 1959, and another large group gathered for the festivities.

Presently this church is affiliated with the Adirondack Parish, which means that they share a minister with two other small parishes in the area. Students from Paul Smith's College add to the attendance now and consistently help the present-day congregation in many ways.

Ministers who have served this church over the years are:

The Reverend:	Dates of Service
William B. Lusk	1897-1906
Thomas B. Anderson	1908-1918
William C. Watson	1919-1923
Henry Cousens	1924-1926
William F. Koenig	1926-1933
Ronald M. Straus	1934-1936
Howard D. Pender	1937-1940

Encouraged by Rev. Jesse Corum, the Presbyterians in Gabriels built a church of their own in the center of the community. This little building was dedicated in 1954 and is a part of the Adirondack Parish, which includes the churches at Keeses Mills and Lake Clear.

Resorts

Probably the Town of Brighton would not be as progressive an area, nor as prosperous as it is today, had it not been for the resort business that early developed around the natural assets of the area. Every little boarding house, inn, cottage group, and hotel that developed in the town, touted in a printed folder the wonders that all could enjoy if they came here. Excellent fishing, hunting, clean air, pure water, rare scenery of mountain splendor were the beckoning words even in the early days of Brighton. These same basic attractions are used today in more sophisticated terms. Although abundance of fish and game were claimed in every resort folder, by the early 1900's it was evident that the idea of unlimited fish and game was proving to be not quite true. The Garondah folder of 1900 still claimed that Rainbow Lake and its nearby waters were some of the finest Adirondack waters,

89

but, it also said they were stocked annually. The day is also past when a hunter can take a walk out in the nearby woods and shoot his deer in time for lunch that day. While we can still boast of comparatively clean air, some waters are becoming polluted and even some of the splendor of the scenery has been dimmed . . . all a part of the changes brought by man in our present society.

Wardner's Rainbow Inn

When they first began to take guests at Wardner's, the popular route people would take from New York City was up the Hudson River, then through the Northern Canal into Lake Champlain where they could get a steamer and then they would get off at Port Kent. At Port Kent they would take a stage coach that followed the Military Turnpike to Paul Smiths. "The Rainbow Inn is reached by private conveyance from Bloomingdale, or if notice be sent in advance, the proprietor will meet the stage at a point four and one half miles on the road to Paul Smiths." Thus read S. R. Stoddard in his ADIRONDACKS, published in 1880. Sometimes guests would go on to Paul Smiths and then Wardners would send guides and boats to bring the visitors back by boat by way of Osgood, Jones Pond, and a short carry into Rainbow. When the Delaware & Hudson was extended to Ausable Forks about 1874, Fitch O'Brien began making three trips a week. Since the train arrived in early morning, it was possible to reach Rainbow that evening.

The earliest name for Wardner's place of business is sometimes referred to as the Rainbow House. This was built in the early 1860's and was a building 92 by 48 feet, two stories high, with broad porches around the house on three sides. There were accommodations for 50 guests with the inside reported to be attractively finished with native woods. It was a substantial building, with large rooms, high ceilings, with plenty of windows for good light and ventilation. There was also a heating system so that it could be heated throughout in the cool weather, such as early fishermen and fall hunters would experience. All this sounds very comfortable for the guests who came at a rate of $1.50 per day or $8.00 a week. The mailing address at this time was Bloomingdale.

Stoddard described James Wardner as a "veteran hunter, who possesses from experience, a thorough knowledge of the surrounding country." This was very true for James Wardner had been in this same area since 1854 when he and his brother Seth had come to the area to hunt and trap while James recovered his health. This knowledge was most valuable and he made it readily available to his guests. Stoddard reported that Mrs. Wardner had placed a number of native birds and animals around the house and he credited her, along with her other accomplishments, with being an excellent taxidermist responsible for their mounting.

By 1894 the name Rainbow Inn was apparently well known for E. R. Wallace in his *Descriptive Guide to the Adirondacks* wrote: "Rainbow Inn, Wardner's forest home." He credited it as eminently calculated to answer the requirements of the seekers after health, sport or scenic beauty. People who wanted to avoid the bustle and expense of the larger hotels were urged to go there. The table was recommended as being bountiful and substantial, with fresh eggs, milk, butter and vegetables from a connected farm. At this time the capacity had been increased to 60 and could boast that the Post Office was right in the house (Rainbow Lake, N. Y.). By this time the Adirondack and St. Lawrence Railroad had a station within two minutes walk of the Inn, or if the guest was coming on the Chateaugay Railroad the Wardner carriage would meet that train if so notified, for the three-mile ride back to the Inn. It is interesting to note that Wallace said that Rainbow Lake had been stocked with trout for the past six years.

With the increase in the number of people coming to the Inn, it had long since ceased to be a one-man operation. Descriptions stated that boats, guides and camping supplies were obtainable at the Inn. It appears that guests were made comfortable in neat, pleasant, home-like atmosphere whether they came for pure relaxation or for sport.

The Inn was nicely situated on a grassy knoll with the bank sloping down to the lake. A brook ran through the grounds and from the hotel porches a colorful garden of flowers could be seen on the slope leading to the lake. For several years these gardens were under the direction of Tom O'Neil from New York City. Tom was a florist and a fine gardener with one problem. He drank too much. His employer arranged for him to come to Wardner's and stay during the summer to look after the gardens, knowing full well that he would have to stay "on the wagon." The Inn was a strict temperance hotel. During the six years that he came he made the grounds a show place.

The dam which James built at the lower end of the lake had, over the years, continued to build up more and more water in front of his hotel and this added to the attractiveness of the spot.

One folder, with no date but apparently about 1900, listed S. W. Barnard as Proprietor and William Moore as Manager. By this time the rates had increased to $2.50 and $3.50 a day and $12 to $15 a week. Now you could leave New York on an evening train and arrive at Rainbow Inn the next morning or if you were in Montreal you could leave in the afternoon and arrive that same evening. This folder was suggesting mountain climbing, for the guest armed with a hotel lunch basket; or carriage trips to Paul Smiths, Bloomingdale, Saranac Inn and other regional resorts to visit friends. Trips to Chateaugay Chasm and Malone were further suggestions. At that time they claimed speckled trout to be the best fishing with fly casting and trolling as the method of snaring the wily ones. Trolling for "lakers" was a side issue to fly fishing and considered less sporty. In fact, the folder intimated that trolling was suitable for the ladies. This booklet also promoted the health inducement, stating that this area was higher above sea level and the air more rarefied, uncontaminated by smoke and microbes that abound in more settled communities. It said there were no offensive smells, no marshy shores or swales and very few mosquitoes. Water for the Inn was brought from the mountains in wooden pipes five feet underground.

The 1905 edition of Stoddard's Guide still listed S. W. Barnard as Proprietor and the top rate was $17.50 a week.

Financial reverses hit the Inn and it was sold shortly after this time to the International Order of Foresters for a Sanatorium.

Wardner's Rainbow Hall

In eighteen hundred and eighty-three
on a mild mid-winter night,
At Wardner's Rainbow Lake Hotel,
where everything goes right,
The boys and girls turn out this eve
in answer to the call
The light fantastic for to trip
at Wardner's Rainbow Hall.

At Bloomingdale, Vermontville too,
the trip they planned to take
To Wardner's famous Rainbow Hall
at Wardner's Rainbow Lake.
And every stylish maiden
is as graceful as a doll
While tripping o'er the ballroom floor
at Wardner's Rainbow Hall.

From Keese's Mill and Saranac
they make the fastest run,
And all the gang from Paul's come up
to have an evening's fun.
At Franklin Falls and Harriestown
they heed the joyful call,
And all the way from Silver Lake
to Wardner's Rainbow Hall.

The sleighbell's merry ting-a-ling
the evening's stillness break,
Upon this night all highways lead
to Wardner's Rainbow Lake.
To reach this spot of wondrous fame
they ride, they walk and crawl
From miles about they gather here
at Wardner's Rainbow Hall.

They come from halfway from New
York, they come from far and near,
The talk about this grand affair
is all the people hear.
And those who stay away this night
with envy sure will bawl
To think they missed the New Year's
Hop at Wardner's Rainbow Hall.

Vene Pay he saws the violin,
while Flanders toots the horn
To keep them dancing to the strains
until the early morn.
Stand on your feet, pull down your
vest, salute your partner's all!
It's lots of fun we always have
at Wardner's Rainbow Hall.

They chasse with an extra kick,
without a single break,
The boys and girls are here tonight
at Wardner's Rainbow Lake.
It's "elimen left and elimen right!"
They never stop at all,
This night of bliss we'll ne'er forget
at Wardner's Rainbow Hall.

Here's Pete O'Malley, just the boy
to superintend the floor,
And if they get unruly he will
sling them through the door.
"Grand right and left" with nimble
feet and "Swing your partner's all!"
They shave her down and shave her up
at Wardner's Rainbow Hall.

Now Warren Flanders calls it off
to keep them on the run,
While Captain Pierce with graceful
glides contributes to the fun.
Both Henry Smith and Burt McCann
are swept against the wall
By all this multitude of sports
at Wardner's Rainbow Hall.

Here Guard Maloney leads the pace
with Jim O'Malley's aid;
To double shuffle around the room
they're really not afraid.
Duck Derby dances in a race
with big Will Pay so tall,
And Robert Coolon referees
at Wardner's Rainbow Hall.

They dance the old year off the earth
and dance the new year in,
Until from hunger every one
becomes extremely thin
The boys consume some juice of rye;
then hasten to partake
Of tempting foods they serve this night
at Wardner's Rainbow Lake.
For such a wholesome midnight feast
they simply have to fall,
Then hurry back some more to dance
in Wardner's Rainbow Hall.

The Devil's Dream, the Irish Trot
and Money Musk they play
To twenty dozen boys and girls
until the break of day.
When morning comes this merry
crowd the journey homeward take
With pleasant thoughts of Rainbow
Hall and Wardner's Rainbow Lake.

94

Garondah Cottage

Not far from Rainbow Inn, on the same side of the road, the Garondah Cottage was built in 1885 with a capacity of 20 guests. This was a three-story cottage, with porches on three sides but was built on the highway rather than on the lake. The lake shore was about 200 yards away. The New York Central station was within sight of the Cottage and was a big asset in securing guests, especially since they advertised that they were open all year round. Rates were modest, at $2 to $2.50 a day and $10 to $15 a week. At that time they could boast of a train trip to Montreal in the morning, time to spend in the big city, and a return that same evening. They promoted fishing, hunting, boating and carriage trips to the area spot of interest. It is interesting to note that persons suffering from tuberculosis were not taken. This reflects that the influx of tubercular patients into the area was well on its way and the early fear of these people already established. Herman Prellwitz and wife Lulu were the first owners of Garondah. Lulu (Louise) Wardner was the daughter of James Wardner, the first settler of Rainbow. When her first husband died she married Fred C. Toof and they continued to run the place for several years. In one of their folders the name Garondah was explained as Indian in origin, meaning "among the trees." Later some cottages were added to increase the capacity to 35 by 1913. As early as 1900 it boasted steam heat throughout and electrically lighted rooms. At one time the Post Office was in the Garondah and they had a telephone early. There were five incoming and six outgoing mails daily. After the death of Fred and Lulu about 1915 the place was sold to William Prellwitz for a summer home for his family.

Garondah once again became a fishing resort in 1954 when it was purchased by C. E. Collins who renovated the buildings and cottages to be able to accommodate about 35 guests. The cottages were made into housekeeping units and the main building was operated on the American plan. One of the guests during this time was John Neronsky, who purchased it in 1960. He continued its operation for a few years but has recently split up the 32-acre property into lots and sold off the cottages, in addition to completely altering the main three-story building into a story-and-a-half house.

The Brighton

If you were to dig around in the leaves in the wooded area across the road from the old Rochester home (now Charles Vahsen) you might come across the remain of another boarding house-type resort. This was the Brighton, operated by L. R. Morris, with accommodations for 35 guests. It was one large building with typical porches all around it. From its appearance it would indicate that it was built around 1890. Their folder stated that they had hot water heat in addition to a large fireplace in the main hall. It was lighted by acetylene gas, but there were electric bells in all rooms. There was a phone in the house and they announced eight daily mails. All this was available to the guest for $10 to $15 a week depending on the room they occupied. The Brighton suggested that new people should contact *their references* and listed several people in New York City, two of whom were attached to Tiffany & Co.

In August of 1914, while the family were all away to the Malone Fair, the Brighton burned to the ground and was never rebuilt.

Buena Vista Cottage

Buena Vista Cottage was kept by Mrs. James M. Wardner (from Rainbow Inn). This was where the Orman Doty place is today. It was a quiet home-like place with open fireplaces, pleasant rooms, and home-supplied table.

Wardner Farm Boarding House

Wardner Farm boarding house, operated by Mr. and Mrs. Frank M. Wardner, was located part way up Jones Hill a short distance beyond Buena Vista. The New York Central Railroad listed it on their map of places to go in 1913. Rates were $10 to $12 weekly with a capacity of 15 and they were open from June first until November first. That same folder also suggested Lake Lily Cottages (later known as Pine Lodge) on Jones Pond with the same rates and a capacity of 20. They were open May to October.

Clark-Wardner Camps

Across Rainbow Lake, about opposite the original Rainbow Inn, the son of James Wardner, Charles A. Wardner, had a resort development known as the Clark-Wardner Camps. They were log cabins, frame cottages and tent camps arranged with space between for individual seclusion. They were equipped for simple housekeeping with dishes, cooking utensils, furniture, spring beds, mattresses and pillows. Campers were given the suggestion of bringing their own silver, linen and blankets. If you did not wish to get your own meals it was possible to take your meals at the main camp. They were located on high ground overlooking Rainbow Inlet and, across the lake, the Post Office and railroad were just a mile away. An improved dirt road leading from the main road made it possible to drive a car to the camps.

The people who came to Clark-Wardner's were of the type that loved nature, enjoyed the many canoe trips possible, and in general delighted in the quiet cultural

97

people who gathered there during the summer. Their advertisement promised that no consumptives or other invalids would be accepted.

The main building, called Nokomis Lodge, contained the dining room and the main household. For years they boasted of their good food served at the camp table. They made mention of the fishing available but did not stress that aspect of their camp. Apparently they encouraged peace and quiet, for the folder told of the implied regulation that all should become quiet at ten o'clock each night and for the rest hour after the mid-day meal. Campers were warned not to bring guns in the summer months, and dogs were never welcome. At 7:30 A.M. the rising bell was sounded with the breakfast bell being rung at 8 A.M. The heaviest meal of the day was served at 12:30 but the supper served at 6 P.M. was nearly as large. The modest rates in 1923 for room and board were $3 a day or $17.50 per week and up.

Development of this resort began in 1899 when title to a large tract of wild forest land was secured. It included a mile of shore on the part of Rainbow Lake known as the "flow" or "inlet." Early in 1901 Charles Wardner began to take lumber and other building materials across the lake in small rowboats. Everything also had to be carried up a winding path from the landing. As he worked on the building he decided to call it Eagle Bay Camp. It was rented for the season almost before the place was finished. More requests for places to rent prompted the next building called Camp Pilgrim. Before the kitchen was even built they moved in and lived in it while construction went on. As soon as it was completed it was rented and they began Inglenook, living in that while building. This one was made of logs cut in their woods and set upon a stone foundation from stones gathered in the area. And so it continued; more cottages, widely spaced for privacy, and more land added until

98

by 1926 they had 200 acres. Pure spring water in a gravity-fed system came from the nearby mountainside. The walking trail around the lake was used first in going and coming; then it was widened for a wagon road; and finally made into a good road that autos could use. Total capacity was finally set at accommodations for 50 people plus the six guest rooms in Nakomis Lodge. Charlie retired in 1952 but members of the family kept it running for several more years. It has been split up now and while the family uses several of the cottages each summer, other camps have been sold.

Northbrook

Northbrook was sold in 1949 by the owner, Rudolph S. Reese, to Edward Sherman who started to make it into a deluxe summer lodge for guests. Originally a Dr. McDougal from Canada had built this as a summer home for himself. This ten-acre property is nicely situated on Osgood Lake, not far off the main highway and on a delightful spot that boasts a lovely view. The three-quarter-mile frontage is a peninsula with the main lodge and several residence buildings scattered over the area. Nothing really ever came of this venture and it was sold again in 1952 to William Schwartau who did some remodeling and modernizing. Mr. Schwartau has room for 30 guests and the fine dining room is well known. Weddings receptions and private parties find the place delightful.

Paul Smith's Hotel

Without a question the most renowned, the most popular and the most fashionable hotel in the Adirondacks was the Paul Smith's Hotel. Some writers even place it in the world-famous category. Certainly it was the largest operation in the Town of Brighton and, even though other factors contributed, it was very largely responsible for the growth of the town.

Much was published in newspapers and magazines about the hotel but most of it was not very helpful in reconstructing a picture of the establishment, as it was on the inside. Several pictures of the building at different periods give us an idea of outside appearance and of its size.

The Town of Brighton was just being formed the year Apollos A. Smith acted on the urging of some of his guests at Hunters Home in Loon Lake to relocate his establishment on the shores of Follensby Pond, later called St. Regis. Dr. Hezekiah B. Loomis, one of the guests, offered to back him in the construction of the new house if Paul would make the place large enough so that the men could bring their wives on these hunting and fishing trips. Paul bought 50 acres of land from Keese & Tomlinson at $6 an acre but, since that was all the money he had, he borrowed $13,000 from Dr. Loomis to build a 17-room house that also included a large living room.

It was in December, 1858, when Paul began his building and by spring he had it finished enough to move into. He married Lydia Martin of Franklin Falls in May, and brought his bride to the place that they were to make world-famous before the turn of the century. The story is told that their first guests arrived a few days after the newlyweds took up housekeeping, in this house that stood on a high sand ridge about 15 feet above the level of the lake, surrounded by pines that were virgin timber. It was, according to Seaver, a primitive building, little more than a shack. But the description given by Dr. Trudeau when he came fifteen years later in 1873 states that while it was primitive, it was most comfortable and clean, with good beds. There was no running water in the hotel, but excellent cool spring water was available from the spring under the bank. Mrs. Smith supervised what cooking she did not do herself, and the food was both abundant and good.

This marriage was a happy combination that proved unbeatable in making the hotel a success from the start. Paul Smith was a happy host, who loved his work of hunting and fishing and, while he lacked formal education, he had plenty of good common sense. He also liked people, and while he was a good listener he could also entertain his guests with his own well-told yarn. Mrs. Smith's influence was evident throughout for she kept the place clean, comfortable and homelike. At first she did most of the work but, as the venture expanded, her job was in supervising the work. No finer table was found anywhere and the service was considered excellent, all for $10 a week at first. Lydia had been fortunate in having considerably more education than was the custom, and she was the one who took care of the books and accounts from the very beginning.

Just when the telegraph came to Paul Smith's Hotel, I don't know. But it was there in 1874 when Trudeau spent the winter with the Smith family. In his *Autobiography*, he told of learning the Morse Code so that he might converse with the operator in Plattsburgh during the long winter evenings. Apparently the hotel kept an operator in the summer, but when he left in the fall there was no contact with the outside world again until spring. Trudeau, through the Plattsburgh operator, kept up on all the outside news that winter. It was known that the telegraph was brought in especially for the hotel. John Harding came to Smith's as telegraph operator in 1878 as a young man of sixteen years. He became a strong friend of the family from that date and Lydia treated him as one of the family. John Harding later owned the Algonquin Hotel in Saranac Lake, and he is buried next to the Smith family in the St. John in the Wilderness Cemetery.

By this time the hotel employed quite a number of guides and stories are told of them gathering at the boathouse, which was on the lake shore. Here they would wait for their parties to start out for a day of sport. There was also a horse barn and several horses.

In May of 1877 the hotel was threatened by a fire in the dry woods nearby. A strong south wind started blowing the fire toward the hotel and by noon the smoke was so bad that it was dark around the grounds. The Smith's were so alarmed that they began moving their most valued possessions to the shore of the lake. Some of the people did put out into the water to keep safe. Sparks kept falling on the barn roof nearby and the guides set up a bucket line. It was fortunate that the wind shifted in the late afternoon and began to blow the fire away from the hotel.

At first the nearest Post Office was in Bloomingdale and mail came only once a week by stage. In 1870 Smith's became a Post Office with Paul as Postmaster. But this must have been a summer arrangement only, for Trudeau wrote of sending three times a week for the mail by sleigh to Bloomingdale, during the winter of '74 that he spent with the family. The official Post Office records show the postmaster appointment of Paul as beginning in 1881.

The Civil War was most profitable for the Smiths. Those wealthy enough to hire someone to fight for them sought to find entertainment for themselves in the various sporting activities offered by the Smiths. Paul not only was able to pay off his mortgages, but accumulated a considerable surplus. He used this money to enlarge and improve his place of business and also to purchase more land. The account of his land deals is a story in itself. In all he accumulated 30,000 to 40,000 acres around and close to his original fifty acres. Some of this land he sold as camp sites to the wealthy families who came, first to his hotel, and falling under the spell of its Adirondack location, wanted places of their own.

As the business grew, the original building became too small so additions were made to it until it became an enormous one. It was never very beautiful as architecture went, being the result of several years of construction. Some parts of it were luxurious, however. Undeniably, the attraction for the great number of people who came, was, in the last analysis, the owners themselves. People found Lydia a fine person to know; one who not only made them feel welcome, but one who by her manner gave dignity to the establishment. Of course, Paul was the all-dominant personality with his wit, charm and limitless stories.

Stoddard, in his book *"Adirondacks"* published in 1880, gave a most graphic description. "Paul Smith's is a surprise to everybody; an astonishing mixture of fish, fashion, pianos and puppies. Brussels carpeting and cowhide boots; surrounded by a dense forest; out of the way of all travel save that which is its own; near the best hunting and fishing grounds, with all modern appliances, and a table that is seldom equalled in the best of city hotels, set right down in the midst of a howling wilderness. While without the noble buck crashes through the tangled forest; within, his noble namesake straddles elegantly over the billiard tables and talks of horses. Out on the lake the theoretical veteran fisherman casts all manner of flies; while in the parlors the contents of huge Saratoga trunks are scientifically displayed, and nets are spread for different kinds of fish. Poodles and pointers, hounds, setters, dandies and other species are found. Feathers and fishing rods, point lace and pint bottles, embryo Nimrods, who never knew a more destructive weapon than a yard stick, hung all around with revolvers and game bags, cartridge pouches and sporting guns."

By 1880 the hotel was four stories high and contained

103

175 sleeping rooms, many of the suite variety, and they advertised accommodations for 300. Besides this there was a larger guide house, now, with space for 100 boats and guides. Since some of the guests brought their own horses there was a fine stable for their use. It was well known that Paul was a connoisseur of horse-flesh and his private stable could prove it.

Charles E. Martin was then manager. He was Lydia's brother. At this period guests were given the suggestion of coming to Paul Smiths from New York City (many, many came from there) by way of the Delaware & Hudson Railroad to Plattsburgh. The Delaware had sleeping coaches so that if they did this and had their breakfast in Plattsburgh they could come the rest of the way to Smith's by stage coach, arriving at 5 P.M.

To attract those not interested in hunting and fishing, several excursions were available to the guest for a modest fee. One might visit Prospect House on Upper Saranac Lake for $1.00; Corey's or Bartlett's $2.00; Martin's for $3.00. A real bargain was a visit to St. Regis Mountain by way of the river to Keeses Mills with a guide to the top of the mountain and return for $1.00, and it only cost $1.25 to do the same trip by way of Spectacle Ponds, Upper St. Regis Lakes and Spitfire. A real luxury item was the rental of saddle horses to carry parties to the top of St. Regis Mountain. No price was given for this trip.

One of the first pieces of property that Paul sold was to Dr. Loomis who built a large, richly furnished cottage to the west of the Hotel. The family occupied this during the season but had most of their meals in the Hotel. He repurchased this sometime bfore 1890.

Several menus were found in the possessions of Phelps Smith after he died and the following is a sample of a dinner:

Paul Smith Hotel — Menu — Dec. 25, 1887

Raw Oysters

SOUP

Chicken with Rice   Clear Consomme

FISH

Boiled Salmon, Hollandaise Sauce

BOILED

Cold Ham   Mutton, Caper Sauce   Chicken, Cream Sauce

ROAST

Beef, Dish Gravy   Turkey, Currant Jelly
Pork. Applesauce   Lamb, Mint Sauce

ENTREES

Chicken Pie   Cream Fritters, Powdered Sugar
Boiled Tongue, Mushroom Sauce

VEGETABLES

Potatoes, Boiled & Mashed   Stewed Tomatoes   Succotash
Corn   Celery   Peas   Boiled Onions

RELISHES

Pickled Tomatoes   Hot Slaw   Spiced Plums
Sardines with lemon

PASTRY

Apple, Mince, Cranberry, Pumpkin Pie
English Plum Pudding, Brandy Sauce   Sago Pudding with Cream
Charlotte Rousse   Jelly Tarts   Macaroons   Kisses
Assorted Cake   Lady Fingers   Lemon Jelly   Wine Jelly

DESSERT

Assorted Nuts   Malaga Raisins   Oranges
Grapes   Figs   Apples

Green Tea   Black Tea   Coffee   English Breakfast Tea   Chocolate

Euclid C. Pine was one of the early managers of the Hotel but he was gone by the later part of the 1880's.

An interesting entry in Mrs. Harold P. Stokes' diary for September 20, 1885, noted that "still 250 people at the Hotel." She wrote that on Sunday the slough was gay with the flags of boats large and small on their way to the hotel docks from which the people had only a short walk to the log church, St. John's, dedicated in 1877. The Stokes' would invite the clergymen to spend Saturday night on Birch Island in Upper St. Regis Lake, to be sure he could arrive in time for services. Mr. Stokes would sail the minister over to Sunday services.

Paul Smith built and maintained a boardwalk that took you dry shod all the way to the church nearby. It was a great convenience, for the road was sandy or muddy, depending on the weather.

While many improvements to his original hotel had been made during the eighties, the biggest changes came after the Paul Smith's Hotel Company was organized on December 12, 1890. Paul, his wife Lydia, and his three sons, Paul, Jr., Henry and Phelps, formed the company and from this date until 1905 the progress was indeed remarkable. The basic hotel was greatly enlarged with a connecting annex to accommodate 500. A new store was built. This store was something to see. Here you could buy clothing, camping equipment, foodstuff, drugstore medicine, hardware, souvenirs, too many items to mention. There was a lovely soda fountain on the main floor, lakeside of the building. It is still in use as a store by the College. Several shop facilities — machine shop, plumbing, etc., two three-story dormitories for help, one for women and the other for men. The stables now had room for 60 horses, and there was a four-story warehouse, a boiler house, launch house, a laundry, woodsheds, saw mill, planing mill, and an office building with winter quarters for the family (Smith cotage). A beautiful three-story casino building 175 ft. x 50 ft. was constructed on the shore of the lake. This had a bowling alley, pool room, grill room, private dining rooms and a kitchen, not to mention a stock exchange office with a direct wire to the New York Stock Exchange on the second floor. Bachelor apartments en suite with private baths were on the third floor and at the lake level were boat slips and landings. It was furnished throughout with mission furniture. There were asphalt tennis courts and they had their own baseball team with games twice a week for guests' enjoyment.

There were many folders put out on the hotel, and one, though undated, must have been printed early in the big expansion period. In this one rates were listed as five to eight dollars a day, American Plan, and chauffeurs would be accommodated for four dollars a day. Paul's Hotel park consisted of 30,000 acres and ten lakes with 23 miles of navigable water. At this time there were 15 cottages; several of these, such as Glover and Harriman, were available on either housekeeping of full hotel service basis. In Glover there were five bedrooms, two baths, living room, dining room, kitchen, and two beautiful fireplaces. Porches were all around. Turner Cottage was to the left of the hotel and had a living room with fireplace, two bedrooms and a bath; Milbank — living room, three bedrooms and bath; Morgan — living room, five bedrooms and two baths; Lambert — living room, seven bedrooms and seven baths; Fletcher—living room, with fireplace, three bedrooms and a bath; Harriman — living room, six bedrooms, three baths, and three fireplaces. Turner, Morgan and McAlpin were on the shore, to the left of the store, while Lambert, Milbank and Fletcher were on the slope back of the hotel and to the right.

Some of these cottages were built for particular guests who specified the architecture and interior design they desired. Sometime later a small cottage was constructed for Irving Berlin near Kellogg. It was from this cottage that Berlin proceeded to woo Ellen MacKay by way of the telephone between the hours of midnight and 3 A.M. Miss MacKay was the daughter of Clarence MacKay, president of Postal Telegraph, and he did not approve of Berlin as a prospective son-in-law.

Wallace in his *Descriptive Guide to Adirondacks* of 1894, called the hotel quarters "luxurious," the meals "epicurean" and stated that "from the beginning it had been a most fashionable resort, commanding the patronage of wealthy people." In passing he listed a barber shop, a service which had been available for some time.

The hotel garden was a showplace, filled with all kinds of vegetables. It was located beside the road, near the Episcopal Church, atop the hill frequently called garden hill.

The newspaper in Saranac Lake carried an article in June, 1894, that listed the official opening as June 15th for the hotel, but among the early arrivals were Dr. Trudeau, William G. Rockefeller (oil), Roswell P. Mitler (Chicago railroader), P. C. Moffit (St. Louis, Mo.), C. C. Glover (Washington, D.C.), A. J. Milbank (N.Y.), H. M. Twombly (son-in-law of Cornelius Vanderbilt), the Robert Hoe's (printing press). The article noted that this was the first season for electric light system with 3,000 incandescent lights inside and 200 arc lights on the grounds. The hotel had a French chef about this time.

The Hotel Company developed several sidelines. One was the sawmill that turned out 50,000 feet of lumber a day, from his wooded acreage. The New York State Forest Commission reports show that in 1894 he cut 150,000 feet of spruce and a like amount of pine. Reports for 1895 and '96 listed the same amounts. They also produced 150,000 shingles in each of those years. Many of the wealthy people who bought land from Smith also bought the lumber to build their lavish camps. When it came to basic furnishings, for the camps, his store was well supplied. He established a local telephone system of about 100 instruments (in 1915) with long distance connections. In this he not only provided a service for the hotel guests but to the local residents who desired the phone installed . . . all at a profit. There had been telegraph service since the 1870's. From early days of guides and rowboats he progressed to sailboats, electric and steam launches as well as guides . . . all for hire. Horses for hire gave way to the garage for storage and repair and cars for hire. The golf course was first placed far enough from the hotel so that transportation to the course was necessary, and for a fee he supplied this too. Water for the hotel and cottages came from a spring 1,584 feet above tide water. It was remarkably pure and so good that they sold it in large bottles which they shipped crated.

A separate company was formed for the development of electric power shortly after the initial Keeses Mill installation. In 1900 he purchased two undeveloped water rights on the Franklin River (Franklin and Union) where he built a 5,000 horsepower generating plant with transmission lines that furnished power for Ausable Forks, Bloomingdale, Saranac Lake, all of the Town of Brighton, and some of the adjacent towns.

In 1906 he began operating a seven-mile electric railroad connecting the hotel grounds with the New York Central's lines at Lake Clear. He had built this on his own land so that he could advertise railroad service to the front door of his hotel. This also made it possible for guests arriving in their private railroad cars to come directly to the hotel with the cars, instead of having to leave them at Lake Clear. He had a siding made especially for these private cars. As better highways were built and automobiles became more abundant, the patrons found little use for this railroad line and it was abandoned in 1932.

The *Adirondack Enterprise* carried a description of the main entrance in July, 1912, and it read as follows: "The door at Paul Smiths, 2 feet six inches by six feet for 53 years, was just changed." The story is told of Grover Cleveland who, in 1884, came on it broadside, became wedged and finally turned and entered it sideways. In each hand he carried a string of trout, which was one reason he shouldered in. The door was so low that "Big Jim" Cross, who stood 6 foot 4 inches in moccasins, always took off his hat and made a definite bow when he entered. Two hat boxes with a bell boy between them caused a congestion that amounted to damages of over $200 to the hats. Originally the door was intended to prevent guides from walking right in the midst of the summer boarders with pack baskets on their shoulders. Therefore, for over a half century there had to be a single file of the thousands who passed through the door.

It was in front of this door in 1870 that P. T. Barnum was hailed by two Italians with an organ and dancing bear. At that time Paul Smiths was fifty miles from the railroad and the men had come footing it through the sparsely settled country to show the trained bear. Paul Smith saw the men first and warned them that in this area folks shot bears and that they might lose him if not careful. Then he told them about Barnum being at the hotel and what he looked like and got them to put on an act. Barnum was flattered that the men should come all that distance and asked the two Italians to see him in New York City.

In the fall of 1914 the last vestige of the stagecoach days was removed at Paul Smiths. New stables were built in the notch in the hill back of the freight house. A news story stated that "the present carriage barn and stables have been on the main drive at the entrance to the grounds for over forty years, and were the scene (until the railroad was built in 1906) of much activity of six jet-black horses and six dead-white ones that drew the coach from the distant railroad station to the hotel. They had yanked the big Concord coach at the crack of George Meserve's whip. When the railroad arrived the coach was abandoned. Now they will be removed from the center of the grounds. A garage will be built for cars and chauffeurs."

In 1916 and 1917 an addition was constructed to the hotel with more bathrooms. A grill room was also built on the ground floor of the hotel.

A New York Central folder of 1913 listed rates at Smiths at $25 and up weekly — the most costly place to stay in the area. The figure of $25 was for chauffeurs and nowhere was mention made of the cost of their better accommodations.

In the 67th year of operation (1925) the summer folder told of weekly tournaments of golf with prizes and cups. Afternoon tea was served daily at the golf clubhouse which guests could reach either by boat or car. It stated that every room of the hotel plus the second and third floors of the Casino had steam heat and a bath attached, electric lights of course. Apartments were available "en suite." All five floors of the hotel had electric elevator service. The annex was connected by a passageway on each floor. The "a la carte grill" was on the first floor and it had a dance floor for afternoon and evening dancing. There were also special rooms for private dinner parties. The first floor of the Casino was a boat livery, piers for launches, gasoline motor boats, electric launches as well as rowboats and canoes were available for rental.

After the death of Paul in 1912, the remaining sons, Phelps and Paul, Jr., were the management until 1925 when Paul, Jr., sold out his interest because of failing health.

It was on September 5, 1930, that Paul Smith's Hotel, one of the oldest and most popular hotels of the north country, burned to the ground. Fire broke out around noon in the main building and with a 30-mile wind blowing it, spread to the annex. In spite of fire companies from Saranac Lake, Tupper Lake and Lake Placid doing all they could, the building was completely destroyed in a

111

short time. There were only about one hundred guests at the hotel this late in the season and they were placed in the various cottages, all having escaped unharmed. Phelps Smith was in Arizona at the time of the fire and Richard Longtin, manager, estimated the damage at a quarter of a million dollars.

During the fire the telephone girls, Monica Mac-Donald and Genevieve Butler, stayed at their post making calls for help and ringing all the rooms to spread the alarm while Dick Longtin went through the building making sure that all the guests and help were warned of the fire. Some personal belongings were saved but most people were forced to leave the building empty-handed.

Since the fire started in the attic of the annex section of the four-story frame building, it was possible to save some things on the lowest floor before the whole building was engulfed in flame. The fire companies pumped water from the lake and fought from behind soaked mattresses. They were able to contain the fire so that it did not spread to other buildings and the nearby woods.

One of the items saved was the treasured oil painting of old Paul Smith and when the crowd, gathered to watch the fire, saw someone carrying this out, a cheer went up from the watchers.

The following year work was begun on the conversion of the Casino building on the lake shore into a hotel. Bert Jay, a stone mason, was employed and he built all the fireplaces and the stone tower on the Casino conversion building. The original Casino was wood and this was jacked up and the stone base put in. The stone tower had a stairwell, elevator shaft and furnace flues. Work progressed slowly on this project as this was depression time after the '29 crash. Although much of the building was completed when Phelps died in 1937 nothing more was done to the building and it was never used as a hotel.

Phelps Smith continued to operate the business until his death in 1937. After the fire, and while the Casino work was going on, the original Smith family cottage (winter quarters) was quickly enlarged and that, plus the cottages, served as the hotel.

When Phelps died, his will directed that his wealth and property be used to establish a co-educational, non-sectarian college at Paul Smiths in memory of his father. While the College did continue to operate the small hotel building for a few years, the advent of World War II and the college activities slowly brought to a close the period of fabulous Paul Smith Hotel days.

Presently, there is nothing left; for fire once again leveled the converted hotel (Smith Cottage) on June 27, 1962, during the time the College was operating it. This time the building was not replaced and that officially ended the Paul Smith's Hotel operation in the Town of Brighton.

McColloms Hotel

McColloms Hotel justly deserved its reputation as a very good place for the sportsman to patronize. Amiel C. McCollom, who started the business, made sure that his guests had good hunting and fishing and he never neglected to serve good food even though the place was certainly not pretentious in any respect.

Situated on the road to Malone in the northern part of the town near Lake Meacham, this simple log hotel, originally built by Amos Rice, seemed to be located in an area of abundant game. Uncle Mac, as he became known, was a fine woodsman and the likeable Scotsman attracted a clientele of zealous sportsmen. He earned the reputation of being the best trainer and judge of deer dogs. This was important, for dogs were the popular method of deer hunting in the last half of the 1800's. As his business ex-

113

panded, he decided to get someone to help him, since all his children died young. His selection of Clarence A. McArthur proved to be a happy choice for the two men seemed to work well together. When McCollom began to feel his age, he took young McArthur into the business with him and eventually Clarence bought him out and greatly enlarged the building, making several improvements. During this time the hotel had several sidelines to provide extra income . . . selling milk, raising hops, and catering to blueberry pickers. Disastser struck in the form of an early morning fire on March 15, 1906. No one was lost in the fire, but nothing was saved of the building or its contents.

It was not too long before McArthur was back in operation for he soon rebuilt a larger hotel from the lumber cut on his own property and sawed in his own mill. The place continued to enjoy its popularity and eventually a nine-hole golf course was added as were several housekeeping cottages. More land was acquired to provide 600 acres of private hunting and fishing. Gradually the type of guest changed from sportsman to family vacationers. During this expansion time, one of his sons, Earl, was helping with the business of running the hotel during the summer season.

When Clarence McArthur died in 1913 it was found that the business was greatly in debt and it was sold under a mortgage foreclosure. Colonel William C. Skinner purchased it from the creditors. The business operation continued, however, under the management of Robert Stevens. After a few years, Earl McArthur was able to regain ownership of his father's property and the family continued to run it for many years. Earl, who was an educator by profession, was a master at the Peddy School in New Jersey. He was able to be home in the summer to operate the hotel in the busy season and his mother and sister, Gladys, ran it during the rest of the year.

Things went along pretty well with the hotel for the next few years; business was reasonably good between the sportsmen and the vacationers, and it was considered to be successful In the early '20's people still went to one place and stayed for their entire vacation. Later on, as cars and roads improved, people did not stay put for an entire vacation and this was responsible for the decline and disappearance of McCollom's and similar small resorts.

Fire struck again early on the morning of June 11, 1924. One of the employees first noticed the fire at 6:20 in the morning and spread the alarm to all the guests so that they were able to escape even though scantily clothed. Most of them had no time to save personal possessions, however. Mrs. F. L. Dunn, sister-in-law of Mrs. Clarence McArthur, became overcome by smoke and had to be carried down a ladder. One of the men got a painful injury when he broke a window to get some of his belongings. He was taken to Rainbow Sanitorium to have the cut sewed up. Gladys McArthur and Claribel Cantwell of Malone tied wet towels around their heads to make their escape from the third floor.

Employees at Meacham Hotel, six miles to the north, noticed the smoke. They contacted the observer at DeBar Mountain and asked him to go to the tower and determine where the fire was. Shortly the observer reported that it was McCollom's Hotel and Robert Stevens, his wife, and their employees started at once to help in the fire-fighting. In the meantime, Gladys McArthur had started for Meacham Hotel to get help and, in her hurry, passed them on the way and failed to recognize them. Practically no one was left at Meacham when she arrived but she did get ladders and buckets and returned home. On her arrival she found that the fire was under control and that the aiding party and guests had saved some furniture and had managed to prevent the fire from

115

spreading to the barn, garage and cottages. It took only forty-five minutes to level the hotel to ashes with an estimated loss of $50,000. They never did find out the cause of the blaze. It was under-insured and the loss to Earl McArthur was heavy. No plans were ever made to rebuild but the family did continue to rent the cabins which stand on the ridge overlooking Osgood River.

Earl McArthur continued in his education work and was the first president of Paul Smith's College from 1937 to 1945. After this the family left the area and the property was sold to Frank Oehmke in 1955, and a bit later to Robert Brown, who is the present owner. It is no longer operated as a resort.

In its day McColloms had several well-known guests such as Arthur F. Rice of the League of American Sportsmen, H. F. Stevens, manufacturer of cotton goods (Utica Stevens sheets and pillowcases), and F. G. Fargo, Wells Fargo Express Co.

Early Campers

According to the assessment records, still on file in the Town Vault, most of the well-known camps on the St. Regis lakes were established from about 1887 to 1895.

1884—F. Lewis Slade
1886—E. Penfold, Col. Payne, Mip Walker, J. A. Webb.
1887—L. B. Smith, E. L. Trudeau, Helen Miller, Grace Mitchell, Whitelaw Reid, C. H. Trask, Charles McBurney.
1888—E. H. Coates, J. L. Depeyster, A. W. Durkee, Susan and Jane Folger, Dr. T. R. French, J. S. Hotchkiss, H. L. Hotchkiss, L. B. Haff (or Hoff), Susan Paton, B. Schlesinger.
1889—Howard Agnew, C. T. Barney, Seraphina Barkley, S. J. Drake, George Earle, Elizabeth Fulton, Alice Huntington, Elinor Munde, Henry Parish, M. Polhemus, Nellie Smith, Whitney, J. C. Cooper, Henry Cranford (on Osgood).
1890—F. Bianchi, Lorenzo Chase, Mary Ewing, J. H. Hopper, Thomas Hockley, H. Twombly.

116

1891—H. J. Brooks, H. Corning, Mrs. M. Livingston.
1892—Mrs. A. H. Dickinson.
1893—E. H. Faulkner.
1894—Mrs. Mary Barber, G. Hoffman, Mrs. G. Rauch.
1895—W. B. Emerson, Kate B. Lee (Osgood).

Some of these campers were well known, both then and now. Simeon Drake was a broker, Ford Huntington of the New York Telephone Company, Whitelaw Reid of the Herald Tribune, Robert Garrett of the Baltimore & Ohio Railroad, S. R. Malinson who was the silk king, Henry Hotchkiss of U.S. Rubber, and F. L. Slade, a prominent lumberman. Dr. Trudeau was one of several doctors who came, but he stayed and his family is still in the area continuing work in the medical field.

When these early campers began coming, they first lived in tents until some time later they completed construction on their buildings. This was the case of Henry Cranford, who bought an island in Osgood Lake which he named Birch Island. His granddaughter, Margaret Cranford, told me that he very nearly chose the White Pine site but the island was the choice when all the family was consulted. The buildings were started in May of 1889, but they lived in a tent for some time. All the supplies were carried from the mainland to the island in a big flat boat called a skow.

Margaret recalls that when they went to a store it was at Paul Smiths, for that was the only one except for those in Saranac Lake. There was a trail through the woods from Osgood that came out near where the College gym is now. They came to the store for all their needs — dry goods, groceries — it was a regular country store with everything available. On the corner where the gym is now, the St. Regis Indians had a sort of stand and they sold baskets of all kinds. As a two-year-old, this made a big impression on her and she never forgot the experience.

For their meats they went to the cooler building, and ice was secured from an ice house just beyond the cooler.

White Pine Camp

Irwin Kirkwood, publisher of the Kansas City *Star,* spent over $500,000 in building this lovely camp on Osgood. There were 26 buildings constructed of rough-sawed planking (brainstorm) so as to blend with the setting. The inside of each building was finished in the finest manner and carefully furnished with all modern conveniences of the time. The living room was 48 x 68 with a beautiful fireplace. Individual cottages provided accommodations for 24 guests. There was a lovely Japanese tea house built on a peninsula of land and reached by a long wooden bridge cutting across a small bay and then finally over a tiny arched bridge. There were two greenhouses for growing cut flowers, and rhododendrons were lavishly planted around the grounds. The tennis courts were of English clay and a fine bowling alley as well as several boat houses. All roads and paths were hard-surfaced.

All this was at the disposal of Calvin Coolidge when he chose this spot for his summer retreat in 1926. This was during prohibition times so the beautiful bar in cabin No. 5 was locked tight.

Grover Cleveland was reported to have spent time at the camp for he was an intimate friend of Archibald White, builder of the camp. He would arrive at the railroad station carrying a small bag and ride horseback to the camp.

Camp Regis

The Camp Regis property was purchased during the late winter of 1946 by Earl Humes and his wife, Pauline. They opened their first year with an enrollment of 72

118

Paul Smith's Hotel, north side, showing the annex joined to the main building by porches. (Circa 1910)

Paul Smith's Hotel, south side, store in foreground. (Circa 1910)

Left to right: Paul Smith's Hotel, girls' building, store, and first casino-boathouse — all from St. Regis Lake.

Harriman and Loomis Cottages in foreground; Paul Smith's Hotel, center; shop, far left; girls' and men's buildings, and warehouse on center road. (Circa 1915)

Paul Smith's Hotel Casino. (Circa 1915)

Paul Smith's sawmill workers about 1895. Fred E. Coulon, in the center, kept the saws filed. His son Eugene is also marked with an "x."

"Pauli" Smith and his brother, Henry, sons of Apollos.

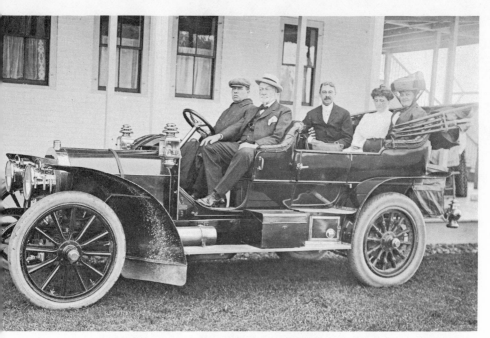

Old Paul Smith and the R. J. Horton family in a Fiat car, August 7, 1909.

Paul Smith in his later years.

Sanatorium; Gabriels, Adirondacks, N. Y.
May 1905, after spending $155 000 Dollars.

Began work in 1895 with $ 15.

Gabriel's Sanatorium, May 1906. (insert) original building.

Rest-A-While cottage at Gabriel's Sanatorium.

St. Margaret's building at Gabriels Sanatorium.

Rainbow Sanatorium, run by the I.O.O.F.

Looking west from the Rainbow Railroad Station was Rainbow San and Garondah Cottage in the distance. Note sidewalk.

Rainbow San — Looking east you could see the railroad station, San farmhouses.

Rainbow San from the lake. The area was all cleared then so you could easily see the lake from the building.

Art Higgins' house and Rainbow Lake Post Office about 1925.

The Machabees Lodge met regularly in the hall over Ben Muncil's garage in Keese's Mills. First row: Roy Otis, Maurice Muncil, Adrian Hyde, Joe Welch. Second row: Tom Burns, John Sawyer, Charles Simpson, Will Titus, B. A. Muncil, Levi Betters, Harry Otis, Jim Titus, Wortley Tyler, unknown, John Jaquis. Back row: unknown, Herb Newell. (Photo courtesy of Gladys Blanchard)

McColloms Hotel

Paul Smith Store and Casino being remodeled (1941) after the big hotel burned.

The Casino, from the lake, during remodeling and before it was removed.

Paul Smith Railway

Phelps Smith, middle son of Apollos, and Watson G. Harding, son of John Harding of early Paul Smith days, and the Algonquin Hotel. Photo taken on Mt. Marcy in 1932.

The Smith Cottage, after it was enlarged.

Brighton Blue Baseball Team about 1948 — Seated: Guy Langloise, outfield; Billy Root, ss; Rube Skeels, c; Tim Sweet, 3b; Wayne Sweet, cf; Butler Sullivan, p. Standing: Art Higgins, treasurer; Stub Goodman, p. and outfield; Harold Carbino, p; Bill Ellithorpe, p; George Fountain, outfield; Perk Tormey, 2b; Bub McGrain, 1b; Bob Gallagher, business manager. Bat-boy, Milton Crate. (Photo courtesy Stub Goodman)

Brighton Town Hall with the War Dead Memorial in foreground.

1690
1732
1776
1792
1825
1858
1861
1892
1912
1937
1964
1971

The famous leaning pine that used to stand on the Paul Smith Hotel grounds.

PAUL SMITH'S FAMOUS LEANING PINE LIVED
THROUGH A LOT OF HISTORY

1690 A white pine seedling began to grow that later became known as the Paul Smith Leaning Pine.
1732 George Washington was born.
1776 Declaration of Independence
1792 First patents in the Alexander Macomb purchased in Franklin County.
1825 Apollos A. Smith was born.
1858 Keeses Mills was a lumber town and Paul Smith started to build his hotel on Lower St. Regis Lake.
1861 Civil War began
1892 The Adirondack Railroad began operating between Tupper Lake and Malone — and
      Original act creating Adirondack Park was instituted.
1912 Apollos A. (Paul) Smith died.
1937 Phelps Smith died.
1964 Vietnam War
1971 Leaning Pine chopped down.

Air view of Paul Smith's College, main campus, 1974. Center cleared area was location of earlier hotel building and Smith Cottage, both of which burned. St. Regis Mountain and Lower St. Regis Lake. (Photo by Gray Twombly)

boys and girls, ages seven to fourteen years. The property, which consists of about 60 acres on Upper St. Regis Lake, was built about 1890 by the Penfold family. Following the death of the Penfolds the property was sold to Gail Gardner and Ruth Doing who operated a camp for children and adults with a specialty of voice and modern dance.

At present the combined population of children attending is about 120 with the younger children, ages seven to fourteen, in Camp Regis, and the older ones, ages fourteen to seventeen, in Camp Applejack, really all a part of one camp. There is a staff of about 36 counselors, with groups of 12 children to each cabin. During the more than 25 years of operation, children from a wide variety of backgrounds and religions have come from all over the United States and foreign countries. Both Mr. and Mrs. Humes have had experience as educators on all levels from primary to college and the camp has an excellent reputation.

Lone Pine Camp

Osgood Lake is the home of the William R. Root summer camp for boys known as Lone Pine Camp. William, Sr., began his operation about 1920, and his son, William, has continued the operation since his father's death. There are seventeen acres with 2,000 feet of shore frontage and a total of 15 buildings for the use of the boys who come each summer to participate in the activity of learning. Both father and son were well educated and members of the teaching profession.

The facilities provided for the campers include cabins, heated by wood stoves, a dining cabin, recreation building that has a library, as well as pool, ping-pong, and other games, a study hall, and infirmary. Back in 1933 one of the parents donated a brand new 1933 Reo

Speed Wagon and that wagon is still used to bring boys to local baseball fields and on other trips. It has become a sort of trademark now that it is so old. All types of learning, both academic and practical, is the rule of the day during the seven weeks that start each year early in July.

Adirondack Swim Camp

The Adirondack Swim Camp originated in 1944 by Joseph C. Reiners and his wife, Carol, of Rochester, N. Y. The camp is located on the shore of Jones Pond and extends back to the Rainbow Road. Originally the property had been developed as Boulder Point Camp for girls on land purchased from Ben and Lottie Muncil, long-time residents of the area. Mr. Muncil built most of the buildings.

Mr. Reiners was a physical education teacher and both Reiners' had experience in education and camp work. Swim Camp is set up for boys seven to fifteen and can accommodate 50 to 60 young men for the seven-week program. With a broad plan of sports, crafts, shop, wilderness survival, and special emphasis on all water activities. Trips out of the camp are made from time to time to test their newly-learned skills. Most of the boys come from the Rochester area but word of mouth advertising has brought new campers from as far away as Hawaii, Texas and Belgium.

While Mr. Reiners supervised the camp activities, Mrs. Reiners looked after the food, kitchen, sanitation, infirmary problems, and the office. She was camp "mother" so to speak.

One of the big problems that first year was food. World War II was going on and food was controlled with the Food Stamp system. Many foods were hard to come by and active growing boys needed plenty of food to keep them going. Meat was scarce, so eggs, cheese and milk

120

were used to stretch the meat diet. Mrs. Reiners talks yet
of the fine help rendered by Paul Smith's office that got
them a phone; of Norman's Grocery, which still supplies
the camp; and of Art Higgins, the Rainbow Lake postmaster, who was unofficial good will promoter.

The health of the Camp was first in the care of Dr.
LeRoy Wardner and later by Dr. Harold Greenier. Helen
Tyler, of Vermontville, was the first cook — turning out
mouth-watering hot biscuits, creamed chicken, fresh
pies and cookies. To promote a good breakfast she added
raisins to hot oatmeal and then offered brown sugar for
a further attraction.

After eighteen years the senior Reiner's have turned
the camp over to their son Joe and his wife. Like his father,
Joe teaches physical education so the camp program
continues with the same philosophy of water activity as
well as learning about the open country with an aim of
developing a positive outlook toward the fuller life experience with nature. It takes a staff of about 25 counselors, plus a food crew of about five to run the program,
in addition to the Reiners family.

Gabriels Sanatorium

The Bishop of Ogdensburg Diocese, the Right Reverend Henry Gabriels, was deeply interested in the Sisters
of Mercy and their suggestions for a nursing institution
in this area. Near the end of 1894 he urged the Sisters to
attempt the establishment of this much-needed sanatorium for the cure of tuberculosis in the Adirondacks. So
they began to consider where to locate such an institution, but attempts to purchase land in Saranac Lake,

Lake Placid and Tupper Lake failed because of excessive costs.

Before they really decided against the expensive locations they traveled to New York City, where they had several friends, in an attempt to secure funds and/or land for their project. While there they contacted Dr. Webb and it was not long after that they received final word of a land gift from Dr. Webb and Paul Smith. Dr. Webb sent them up on his train to look over the land. They stayed at Rainbow Inn. Mrs. Wardner met them at the train that November morning they arrived and later Mr. Wardner drove them up to see the plot of land. It was a clear winter morning and the two hills looked so bright and healthful that the Sisters were delighted. The land was surveyed and they received their deed in February.

But it was spring 1895 when the two Sisters ventured into this wilderness of Lot 78 in the Town of Brighton, consisting of one hundred acres, the gift of Paul Smith and Dr. H. Seward Webb, a son-in-law of William H. Vanderbilt. Dr. Webb was the one who was responsible for the New York Central Railroad coming into our area. Their plot was situated close to the railroad on a rolling piece of land that gradually rose to a good-sized hill, which they called "Sunrise Mount." All around them they could see the mountains and toward the back of their land was the beautiful Lake Lucretia, supposedly named this for the New York State architect, I. C. Perry's wife (locally called Jones Pond). Mr. Perry gave the Sisters all manner of assistance in planning the buildings.

With their strong faith to sustain their determination, the Sister M. Perpetual Help Kieran and M. McAuley Connolly, began the first year of their new institution at Gabriels with very little. A friend had built a small cabin for them, while another friend had given them a cart and a donkey. All the Motherhouse could give them was $15.

122

Yet that $15 was increased through their efforts to many times that amount that went into the building of Gabriels Sanatorium, named in honor of their Bishop.

Work on the cellars was begun the last part of April by B. B. Lantry and the contract for the administration building was given to Branch & Callanan of Saranac Lake on August 15, 1895. The contractor had agreed to build the main building, exclusive of the marble, for $10,985.00, and one cottage for $2,955.

The general idea of their plan was to centralize a group of cottages around the administration building This was more expensive to build and maintain, but they felt that this plan would contribute more to patient comfort and health. They spared neither pains nor money to achieve this. The heating, ventilation, plumbing, drainage and water supply were the best that science could provide at that time. Later a Paris Exposition awarded a medal to the San for this arrangement.

The cornerstone of the Sanatorium was placed by the Right Rev. Henry Gabriels on July 6th in the year of our Lord, 1895. Present were Right Rev. Henry Gabriels, Rev. Michael L. Holland, Tupper Lake; Rev. Michael I. Brown, Hogansburg; Very Rev. Thomas E. Walsh, Plattsburgh; Rev. Peter J. Devlin, Chateaugay; Rev. Dennis Nolin, Massena Springs; Rev. Bernard Marron, Potsdam; Daniel Griffin, Watertown; Paul Smith, Sr.; Rev. Mother Stanislaus of the Sisters of Mercy; Sister M. Perpetual Help Kieran, foundress of the Sanatorium.

Work continued that year and the next on the administration building, Rest-a-While and Kiernan Cottage. However, it was not until July 26, 1897, that they were able to take the first patients. With a stated purpose of treatment of incipient cases of pulmonary tuberculosis and certain moderately advanced cases, they began this charitable work. It was a non-sectarian endeavor and no distinction of creed or color was made. One of

123

their early publications stated that 15% of the patients were treated free, only a few paid the entire cost and the greatest number paid less than the per capita cost. When a patient entered the institution they not only were treated for the "great white plague" but they were taught every detail of the prevention so that they might tell others and thus possibly prevent other cases developing.

At first the San Post Office was in B. B. Lantry's store just off the grounds; then it was brought over to the administration building. Soon a portable Post Office was erected close to the road as the people from the neighboring area were afraid of catching TB. The Post Office was obtained through Theodore Roosevelt, and the Sisters were in charge for a number of years.

As this health resort was being built, the little hamlet that grew up around it became known as Gabriels. Prior to this the few families that were there just called it Brighton.

In 1897 Rest-a-While was completed and St. Joseph's came along in 1898, made necessary by the overflow of men patients.

"Slumberland" consisted of ten street cars that were used at the very first for patients. They were placed in an oval with plenty of space between. This was the first Knights of Columbus unit at Gabriels. Each was fitted up with beds, stands and nursing equipment such as hot water bottles.

In 1900 the "Mary D'Arcy Cottage" camp was built for patients who could move about.

The water supply for the San came from springs located on the side of an uninhabited wooded highland. The water came from eighteen wells pumped into a reservoir and was the purest natural water obtainable.

By 1903 a total of $135,000 had been spent on the plant, about half of this amount had been paid but the rest was still a debt. Growing slowly, there was a dozen or so buildings clearly visible from the hamlet of Gabriels, which now had a station on the railroad. There were cottages, a chapel, laundry and heating plant in addition to the other buildings mentioned. They had their own electric light plant and the excellent water supply. They eventually acquired a 200-acre farm, which still is known locally as the Sister's farm.

December, 1903, also brought out the first issue of a quarterly magazine, *Forest Leaves*, which was started by Sister Kieran. Many of the articles were about the San itself, but others were definitely literary or historical. This magazine continued to be published until December, 1934.

Patient rates about this time were from $16 to $22 a week depending on the room, payable weekly, and this included room, board, medical atendance and ordinary nursing. Patients were required to provide themselves with outdoor blankets, fur coats and other suitable outside wraps. Records show that the average length of patient stay was eight months.

Their farm supplied them with all the milk and cream required, most of the eggs needed, chickens and enough turkeys so that they could serve turkey often, as well as veal and pork in moderate quantity. The pigs were fed on sterilized food wastes from the San. All of the bread used was baked here. Some of the Sisters themselves supervised the work on the farm and lived there.

During the year 1914, in order to meet the increased demand for treatment, four abandoned horse-cars were donated by the Metropolitan Street Railway Co. of New York City and were shipped free by the N.Y. Central Lines to serve as temporary shelters for patients. It was also the year that saw the death of Sister M. P. H. Kieran on July 24th.

On January 18, 1916, flames broke out in the attic of the administration building from a defective flue and spread rapidly over the upper part, finally eating its way to the lower stories. There were twenty-five patients in the building when the fire broke out. All were removed to safety and later taken to the Forester's San at Rainbow. With a strong wind blowing, all the rest of the place was seriously threatened. A call went out over the telephone wire to Paul Smiths and every man was gathered from the shops, mills, store, ice cutters and so on . . . all were sent to help fight the fire. All the people along the roads in Gabriels and Rainbow also came to help. When the call for help went to Saranac Lake Fire Department a special train was dispatched with about 50 men, hoses and ladders. It left Saranac at 8:55 and arrived at Gabriels at 9:30. When they had carried all their equipment up to the fire they discovered their hose, which was standard size, would not fit the San hydrants. By this time the building was in ruins and so all efforts were concentrated on keeping the sides and roofs of the other buildings from catching fire.

When the smoke cleared all that was left was the foundation. On that foundation the New York Chapter of Knights of Columbus erected their temporary buildings, units one and two, with space for 18 patients, for the care of sick members of the Council in Manhattan and Bronx. Later this became known as the Priest's Bungalow, where the staff Priest stayed.

Next came the construction of St. Margaret's in 1923 to be followed by the K. of C. units No. 3 and No. 4. Each of the last two units were of fireproof construction and had beds for 22 patients. These units were a part of a state-wide plan for treatment of members. The Edward Smith Memorial Infirmary building came to be built in 1927 through the generosity of George R. Smith and John T. Smith in memory of their brother and father. This was a modern building in all respects and became the principal one since all patients were admitted and remained there until they were ready to become ambulant patients. This building had a minor operating room, laboratory, pharmacy, x-ray and dental departments.

In the San report for the year ending January, 1918, they had admitted a total of 2,442 patients. Many were from New York City and Canada with New Jersey, Ohio, Pennsylvania, Massachusetts, and Rhode Island next in amount, but they came from all over the country and even some came from Cuba. In addition to the nursing Sisters there was a medical staff in attendance. Dr. Henry J. Blankemeyer was the resident physician with his assistants, Drs. Perrin, Milan and Richard.

During the early 1940's the rates had been stablized at $35 weekly, but even then they were running up a deficit. The per capita cost, excluding the value of the Sisters' services, was $5.73 a day. Some of the signs of the future were in this superintendent's report for references were made to help shortage, putting off needed repairs and the struggles to maintain their high standards of care.

By 1946 it was noted that, except for the contribution of the Sisters' services, very little had been received in the way of donations. Most of the generous benefactors of old were all dead. The deficit was so alarming that in September of that year they had to raise the rates slightly. They cut improvements and maintenance to the barest minimum but continued to maintain the high quality of their food and care. Labor shortages had forced them to sell the farm that had been their source of milk, cream, potatoes and other vegetables. The Sisters began to take over double duties in the kitchen and dining room. The patient load, which had fluctuated between 45 and 60 in the early years, had gone to 190 in 1943. The two factors of reduced donations plus greater expense was a serious problem facing the Sisters of Mercy. It was during the '40's that they had for the first time admitted patients other than those with TB, for they had taken in those who needed rest or were recuperating from an illness.

While still caring for tuberculosis patients, in 1954 they began to accept the aged and chronically ill as well as those needing care following some form of hospitalization.

Another fire had also created a further problem. This fire occurred on July 23, 1953, breaking out in the attic of St. Joseph's Convent building. It was occupied by twelve aged and ailing nuns and was completely ruined from the fire. It had been a two and a half story wooden building erected in 1928 and all recently renovated. Firemen worked hard to prevent the fire from spreading. They did confine the damage but little was saved from the Convent itself. Patients in Units 3 and 4 as well as Rest-A-While were real close to the action but none were harmed.

Only nine TB patients remained by 1960 and their new specialty, geriatric care patients, numbered 55. One of the reasons for the decline of TB patients was the general reduction of the need due to the use of the many miracle drugs that had been reducing the numbers of patients in all similar places of treatment such as Trudeau and Stonywold in our immediate area, for example.

This new nursing program called for a re-evaluation of their facilities and it was soon realized that their buildings could not meet the modern requirements. A drive for funds began, with the idea of a new construction program. As the drive progressed it became apparent that a complete relocation would be in the best interests of the program and so the Sisters sold their Gabriels property to Paul Smith's College in September, 1963. During the seventy years they had operated at Gabriels, they had treated over five and a half thousand patients.

Presently the College uses the Gabriels property for student and faculty housing and some classes in forestry are held there. The Sisters have moved to the beautiful Uhline Nursing Home in Lake Placid, where they have continued to provide the very last word in geriatric care.

Rainbow Sanatorium

Rainbow Sanatorium was owned and operated by the Independent Order of Foresters. It was opened on July 20, 1910, with two patients for the free treatment of any of its members suffering from early stages of pulmonary tuberculosis. This was the property that had been purchased a few years earlier from James M. Wardner (Rainbow Inn) and converted into the Sanatorium. It consisted of 600 acres, fifty of which was lake, fifty or more cleared land and the rest in woodland.

There were eight buildings. The main one was three stories, 90 x 45 feet, with a wing to the back for the help. It was equipped with the most modern steam heating plant and electric lights as well as a fire protection system. Facing southeast, it had nine-foot porches running the whole length of the three stories in the front and back. Dining rooms, offices, reception room and sun parlor were on the first floor with sleeping rooms on the two upper floors. Porches were screened in summer and had swinging windows that could be opened in the winter months. There was a cottage on the lake for fifteen patients, a boat house, garage, ice house, dairy barn, hog barn, and a building to house the farm machinery, tools, wagons and sleighs.

The main building stood on the shore on Rainbow Lake, one-eighth of a mile from the Rainbow Station on the Adirondack Division of the New York Central Railroad. Their informational folder stated that the San was

370 miles from New York City, 133 from Utica, 100 from Montreal, 11 from Saranac Lake, and 5 miles from Paul Smiths.

It is interesting to note the statements made relative to the altitude and climate. Quoting: "The altitude at Rainbow is 1,708 feet above sea level. This is sufficient to afford the advantages of elevation without any bad effects. Thus a patient with his disease arrested may return to his home without fear of the unfortunate results which have followed the going from a great elevation to a low level. In summer there may be a few warm days, but the nights are always cool. In winter the temperature at night may go many degrees below zero, but on account of the dryness of the air, the heat in summer and the cold in winter are borne without any discomfort."

During the fall of 1915 the old fence and board walk that ran all the way to the railroad station was removed and a cement walk laid. An ornamental wire fence was also erected. The wire fence can still be seen, and here and there a piece of the sidewalk shows up slightly below the needles and soil that has nearly covered the walk.

In 1920 their annual folder stated that the Post Office had been moved to their farm house, beside the railroad station. An archway had been cut between two rooms in the house, thus giving room for a store, which was run by the station agent, in connection with the Post Office. This is the house presently owned and occupied by Francis Hogan. The Postmaster at that time was Frank F. Coach.

Right after World War I there was apparently a shortage of Forester patients to be able to run the place economically. Consequently, they took advantage of the opportunity to accept "War Risk Soldiers" suffering from tuberculosis. The government did not have room in their hospitals for all their soldiers who needed care so they contracted them out to various sanatoriums. At one point they had 60 to 65 soldiers as patients.

All patients were told that they could be cured only by months, and sometimes years of self-denial, and the most painstaking care to every detail of their daily life. To this end certain rules were laid down and enforced. These included proper food, rest and breathing the pure air of the area. Three meals a day were normally served, with extra milk and eggs in mid-period lunches for some patients. Wine, beer or other alcohol stimulants were not allowed at any time. Smoking or other use of tobacco was forbidden except in very special cases and those had to be approved by the doctor. Cigaretts were always forbidden. In the rare cases where some tobacco use was permitted it would have to be used outdoors. Patients were instructed to spend every possible moment resting out of doors, only remaining indoors to dress, undress, bathe or go to meals. They were expected to spend at least eight hours a day outside. They must be sitting or reclining outside from 8:30 A.M. 'til noon; 1:30 P.M. 'til 5:30 and from 6:30 to 7:30 in the evening. Kalamazoo and Adirondack recliners were used by the patients on the porches. Beds were fitted with large rubber casters that made it possible to move beds on and off porches with ease. Those who were progressing enough to be able to take exercise had from 11:15 A.M. to 12:15 and from 3:30 to 4:30 P.M. Exercise meant walking. Patients sat out on porches in all weather — rain, sleet or cold. They claimed that the Adirondack winter was the best possible time to cure. Patients were bundled up in plenty of warm clothing and blankets so they were warm from head to toe.

In the Sanatorium report for 1920, ten years after opening, they had admitted a total of 642 patients. The first year 102 had come for the cure and after that it was never over 70 until the soldiers came in 1919 and 1920,

131

at which time there were 192 patients. Most of those who came here were from the United States and Canada but quite a few came from foreign countries.

One of the patients who came in 1920 was Matthew Knudson. After his release he stayed on in Rainbow Lake and for many years was an active Justice of Peace until his retirement in 1971. The head nurse, a Mrs. Ziegler, continued to live here for a few years and then finally sold her place to General Russell J. Minty in the 1940's.

The resident physician, Dr. J. Seymour Emans, also contributed his services to the area residents and was the school doctor while he was attached to the San.

In 1934 the few remaining patients were moved to the Foresters San in California and the Rainbow operation was phased out. The William Hogan family purchased the farm part of the property, some of the land was acquired by Carl Anderson, Harry Hull, and Douglas Martin. The boathouse was moved up to the main road and used to make the Higgins residence. The main building was completely torn down so there remains no evidence of the Inn or the Sanatorium. Harry Hull subdivided his section soon after he bought it in May, 1931. Boot Bay area on Rainbow Lake is a part of this subdivision. The Doug Martin acreage is now a part of the Charles Vosburgh subdivision, one of the latest housing developments in Rainbow Lake.

Organizations

The Brighton American Legion Post No. 1397 was formed on February 6, 1946, in a meeting held at the Town Hall. A membership of fifty elected the following officers: Charles O'Dell, Commander; Roger Benton,

1st Vice- Comm.; Halsey Brulliea, 2nd Vice-Comm.; Clarence Rork, 3rd Vice-Comm.; Raldy Martin, Treasurer; Clem Collins, Adjutant; Lawrence Quain, Chaplain; Richard Strack, Historian; Gene Abare, Sgt. at Arms; Robert Gallagher, Service Officer; Lloyd Crary, County Committeeman; and Glenster Sawyer, County Alternate. The Charter was presented at this meeting. Colors were donated by Richard Longtin and Oscar Otis. The gavel and rifles were given by Con Meagher.

Shortly after this, the Post purchased a home in Gabriels, on the main street, for a meeting place and for several years sponsored such activities as a Scout troop, Little League Baseball, and annually conducted a Memorial Day service at the Town Hall. The Post was finally abandoned in 1970 because of the lack of interest and dwindling membership. The final few members decided to join the Saranac Lake Post.

An Auxiliary group was formed late in 1947 and received their Charter in March, 1948. Sixteen members were initiated at his meeting, with Frances Lepine, President. Original members were Frances Lepine, Mary Wilson, Mary Higgins, Jennie Rochester, Pauline Meagher, Maude Muncil, Amy Titus, Mabel Sawyer, Joyce Crary, Mae Martin, Dorcas Tyler, Anna Kelly, Mabel Martin, Florence Brulliea, Ola Gallagher, and Gladys Blanchard. The ladies were instrumental in getting and keeping the Legion Home equipped during the years when it was a popular gathering place. They have raised funds for, and made available, various pieces of equipment for the care of the sick and injured. Holiday gifts and visits to the various hospitals and sanatoriums are made annually and they were constant with their assistance with the Memorial Day service. The Auxiliary continues to function in their service capacity even though the Post has been closed.

Baseball in Brighton

There were baseball games in the summer at Paul Smiths' Hotel. Paul used to hire college boys who could play ball. He gave them some soft job but their main work was playing a good ball game. Considerable enthusiasm was developed over the rival team in Saranac Lake at the Ampersand Hotel. It sort of worked out that Paul hired Yale men and the Ampersand hired the Harvard fellows.

The Brighton Blue baseball team provided many thrilling games during the years they played in the Northern League. It was little wonder that the Blue were League winners for several years when the fans packed the bleachers in the late 1940's and early '50's. The field at Gabriels was reported to be the best in the League and night games were especially popular when they got lights in 1949.

Interest in baseball waned when a pro team was brought in to play in the mid-1950's. The local people had come to see the hometown boys play; and when they were not the attraction, the fans did not come out. So after a few seasons of pro games, baseball disappeared except for our Little League teams. The field is still good but the bleachers and lights are gone.

Rainbow Lake Associates, Inc.

The first attempt to form an organization of the residents of the Lake was made in 1924 with a constitution, by-laws and a code of ethics. The water level of the lake was a prime concern at the time as was some of our current problems such as fish stocking, observation of game laws, and prevention of fires. They called themselves the Rainbow Lake Association and while they did accomplish a name change from Rainbow to Rainbow Lake for the railroad station, they were not too successful in controlling the lake level.

For several years prior to the formation of *Rainbow Lake Associates, Inc,.* there existed a very unsatisfactory control of the water level of Rainbow Lake and adjacent waters. At times the level of the lake dropped many inches, badly affecting the camps at the upper end of the lake. The lower end was also inconvenienced, but not as much. At that time the International Paper Co. controlled the water level by means of the Lake Kushaqua Dam. Several property owners (Wardner, Hochhausen, Donovan) had certain agreements with the paper company, supposedly protecting their "rights." The agreements were little protection at best and honored only when the property owners protested the water levels.

The Kushaqua Dam continued to go into disrepair and all efforts to get the paper company to repair it were useless.

In July, 1946, a group of shore owners met to discuss the situation and try to come up with a solution. This discussion led to a second meeting to form a property owners association at which time Col. Brett, H. T. Hochhausen, Charles Wardner, L. W. McFarland, Dr. Edward Carter and Frank Zeraga all subscribed a substantial amount to start a fund to repair the dam if no other means could be found to fight the bad situation. Further funds were sought from all shore owners. This was the beginning of the present organization, growing out of the need to solve a common problem for the shore owners.

By February of 1947 the dam was so bad that the State ordered the Eastern N. Y. Power Co. (successors to Inernational Paper Co.) to repair or remove the dam. They chose to dynamite it. This created a serious problem for Stony Wold Sanatorium and shore owners on the upper end of Rainbow could not use the lake at all. The Association and Stony Wold teamed up to seek cooperation from the power company to build a new dam.

After considerable negotiaion, in 1947 an agreement was reached with the Eastern N. Y. Power Co., who was the owner of the defective dam, to rebuilt it for certain "rights." This contract was signed for the *Associates* and is still in effect. The Company has lived up to their agreement, and since the construction of the new dam, we have enjoyed satisfactory water level. High water in the spring from snow melt is drawn off as fast as possible and everyone can use the lake during all seasons.

Having accomplished their original purpose — securing a new dam — the *Associates* continue to exist to create and promote a communal interest in all that concerns the increasing number of shore owners on the various waterways joined by Rainbow Lake.

Over the years a variety of problems have been considered by the organization. The Rainbow Causeway has been repaired from time to time. In 1954 concern was expressed about fire protection, and the first fire map was drawn up, complete with a set of signals and camp numbers. By 1955 this was an important part of the agreement reached with the Bloomingdale Fire Department, and various contributions have been made to this department since that time. In 1971 the Fire Map was completely redone, printed and distributed. A major point of concern that has not been solved yet is the institution of some type of zoning for the lake property to protect the beauty and health as well as the investment of each shore owner from the possible misuse by indiscriminate people. The *Associates* now have an even larger responsibility with the increasing number shore owners coming along with the development of the Vosburgh Tract. There were 80 shore owners in 1972 and each season has brought several more.

Concern for the natural resources has been evident from the earliest times, with the trial stocking of fish in the first years and frequent consultations with the Conservation Department. Classes in wildlife identification for the children of the Lake were conducted one summer. Guest speakers have appeared at the meetings to inform the membership about sanitation, wildlife, zoning, fire protection,and other current topics. However, the unique floating islands, bogs, or whatever you call them is, and probably always will be, a yearly topic for consideration. As the hot summer weather advances, these islands rise from the depths. Much consideration has been given to their removal, and all schemes, such as weighting them down with stones, or cutting off the stem-like bottoms, have failed.

St. Regis Property Owners' Association, Inc.

The Certificate of Incorporation of the Upper St. Regis Property Owners' Association, Inc., dated August 28, 1915, stated the purpose of the organization as follows:

"The particular objects for which the corporation is formed are to take all necessary steps to promote and improve the beauty, navigation, purity and salubriousness of the Upper St. Regis Lake . . . and to conserve and to promote the interest and comfort of persons owning or occupying camps and cottages upon the shore of such Lake."

This was later amended to include Spitfire and Lower St. Regis and the name was changed to St. Regis Property Association, Inc.

A perusal of the minutes of annual meetings from 1927, when the Property Owners Association and the St. Regis Yacht Club were separated, brings to light certain recurring themes and some special highlights.

Among the perennial concerns: The doctors made annual inspections of the dairy and found practices and

137

conditions so good that for a long time they considered pasteurization unnecessary! The problems of repairs to docks and the Post Office building were no fewer nor any less irksome than they are today . . . only less expensive.

Maintenance of the water level in the lakes. At what level? To suit whom? Increasing concern about speeding motorboats, particularly at night and in the slough. These topics came up each year, as did the unfavorable comments on the telephone service.

The Golf Committee supervised the golf course for some years when the Paul Smith Hotel Co. still maintained it until 1949 when the College could no longer spend its money this way.

The Fish Committee reported repeatedly of fish stocking until it was abolished in 1954 after the State reports for the last few years indicated that "trout fry could not survive" as there was too little oxygen in our shallow waters that were well supplied with enemies.

For some years, something called the Canoe Committee planned and engineered weekly, all-day expeditions to various neighboring lakes and rivers. The members took canoes or guide boats, lunch, cameras, bathing suits, etc., etc., and embarked in a flotilla at some convenient spot; paddled up or down, picnicked and swam, while various guides and others moved the cars to a late afternoon meeting point.

The more recent refrains include these: Buy stamps to keep the Post Office running . . . Park your trailers and "long time" cars in the new Parking Lot at the Landing and leave the landing clear for others.

High spots worth noting: The telephone line from Paul Smiths to Upper St. Regis was operating (1927). The treasurer's report for that year showed eight checks drawn for expenses totaling $811 and an income of $876. Compare this to 1971-'72, with 61 checks, expenses of $3,355 from an income of $4,081.

138

In 1928 Dr. Francis B. Trudeau, Chairman of the Sanitation Commiteee, said "all camps which had unwittingly polluted the lakes with sewage, have now so corrected their sewage systems that no longer are they a menace, and that drains will no longer be a topic of conversation."

In 1932 the Association paid the first school tax to the Town of Harrietstown, $17 (1972 tax $401). The dock area owned by the Association is not in the Town of Brighton, but the largest part of the Association coverage is in the Town of Brighton.)

In 1937 some property at the Landing was purchased in order to make way for a "private road to and across the Carry." A gasoline pump was installed at the Landing. Members agreed to a boat tax to provide for maintenance of docks and parking facilities at the Landing, in 1955.

The following year the organization made arrangements with the Bloomingdale Fire Department for a depot of fire fighting equipment on the lakes. For the next several years the main project was the promotion of efforts towards zoning ordinances in the Town of Brighton and also in Harrietstown.

St. Regis Yacht Club

The first "cup race" on St. Regis Lake took place on July 23, 1885. There were four boats manned by Anson Phelps Stokes, Dr. E. L. Trudeau, C. M. Lea, and Newton Stokes. The race was set for four o'clock; it was a very hot day; and not a hint of a breeze. Later in the day a slight bit of wind came up and they managed to have the race with A. P. Stokes declared the winner. Several races were held that year and at the end of the summer, Mr. Lea took home the cup donated by Mrs. A. P. Stokes.

Informal racing continued but it was not until 1897 that any consideration was given to the formation of a club with set racing rules and regulations. The final step was taken at the Simeon J. Drake camp on Spitfire, September 3, 1897. There were 55 members in 1899 with A. P. Stokes, Commodore; E. L. Trudeau, Vice-Comm.; L. Bayard Smith, Sec.; Simeon J. Drake, Treas.; Samuel V. Hoffman, Measurer.

There was no clubhouse or mooring area . . . each vessel rode at anchor off the owner's camp. Meetings were generally held at the camp of the commodore. In the earliest days, when the finish line was in front of Birch Island, the ladies would gather to watch the conclusion of the various events.

In 1900 the Idem Class sailed their first race. There were seven in the club, all built alike, at an approximate cost of $750. They were 32 ft. long, 19 ft. water line, 8 ft. beam, and rigged with 600 sq. ft. of sail. Whitelaw Reid's *Water Witch* is still afloat on its own tiny sea at the Adirondack Museum at Blue Mountain Lake.

In later years the boat register has 12 Idems; 5 "E" Scows; 19 "O" boats, 4 other sailing yachts, plus 60 motor boats from 16 to 30 feet in length and powered from 45 to 200 horsepower. Many of these were manufactured by Chris-Craft. There were also 13 electric-powered boats.

From the earliest days, the Club was not content to be concerned with encouraging yachting and keeping the channels clear of logs; it also assumed the role of unofficial watchdog over all things for the good of all the people who lived on the St. Regis Lakes. It took strong measures to make sure there would be no pollution by sewage, soap, gas and oil. It fought to keep proper water levels and to make sure that streams were stocked with fish. It even was instrumental in securing the Upper St. Regis post-office.

In 1909 the Yacht Club membership rejected the idea of a second organization to deal with these extra chores, but a few years later it came into being. It was good that a Property Owners Association did come about for World War I brought a halt to racing and the owners became the only active community organization. Even after the war, the Association sponsored informal races until 1927 when the Yacht Club was reactivated, as an affiliated but separate part of the Property Owners Association.

In 1932 the Club accepted a challenge of the Royal St. Lawrence Yacht Club to compete with a series of team races, three to be sailed on Lake St. Louis and three on Upper St. Regis Lake. The Americans won locally but the Canadians took the series. The following year another international contest took place with the same results.

Racing continued each season with great enthusiasm as the younger racers became more and more involved. For many years the season's prizes were given out at a Labor Day tea held at the Slade Camp. Races were suspended again during the second World War, but renewed activity began with the young skippers going over their crafts and coming up with new ideas just as soon as the war was over. When the Club celebrated its fiftieth birthday there were 117 senior and 37 junior members.

Very strict rules cover the operation of motor boats and they are taken very seriously.

Biographies

JAMES M. WARDNER was born in Chesterfield Township near the village of Keeseville, N.Y., on August 15, 1831, according to John H. Titus in his *Adirondack Pioneers*. His father, Nathan J., had a farm there but his main occupation was school teaching as he was badly crippled with rheumatism. His mother was Phoebe and there were several brothers and sisters to help with the farm work. As a young boy he and some friends came part way into this region on a camping trip and he was much attracted to the hunting, trapping and fishing life that he experienced on that trip. He was always a good shot and because of this was hired to go on a wagon train going west when he was nearly eighteen years old. He and a friend took the job to help provide meat with their guns and left with the train early in the summer of 1849. However, a good many factors caused him to change his mind about this venture of going to California for gold and the two boys left the train in early September when they reached Toledo, Ohio. James stayed in Toledo for five years, working at various positions, and while there contracted tuberculosis. The doctor advised that he return home and rest in the clean mountain air.

On his return home, James, his brother Seth and a friend, Lorenzo Rand, made plans to come north into this area where he had heard great tales of the abundance of game. During the period of the preparation for this trip to the mountains, they had made a deal with a wholesale supply company to sell venison to the company dur-

142

ing the cold winter months. So when they had collected all their supplies, the three young men set out for the mountains in search of James' health. James also wanted to locate a good farm site for he had always enjoyed the farm chores at home. They cut through the woods and finally arrived at the Old Military Road, following it to Bloomingdale and on to Saranac Lake and then on over the Harrietstown hill to the home of Lorenzo's father. The father was Alfonzo Rand and his farm was located about where the Young farm is now. The boys camped there for a few days, getting information about land that might be available. A couple of possible sites were discussed and they eventually settled for the first fall and winter on Osgood Pond. In a cleared spot, where possibly John Osgood had tried to settle and probably where the Boy Scout camp was later located. During the fall days of exploration, James investigated a hardwood area and bought 50 acres upon which he built his first rough home, a mere shanty. He had found a lake near his land and named it Rainbow because of its shape. One of the first things he did was to build a sort of road from his property out to the Military Road, a distance of four miles. Next he cleared some land and got it ready to plant. The first winter they spent on Osgood but the following summer (1850) they began to live at the Rainbow site.

His shanty and farm was located on a brook on the southwest shore of the lake he called Rainbow, about where the pine grove is presently growing. The brook is still there. With the hunting contract and his farming he managed to earn a living and gradually built a barn, got a water system in operation, and did some guiding on the side . . . all this while regaining his health. He continued to clear his land for farming and bought another 100 acres from William Ricketson on the south adjoining his land.

His mother, Phoebe, had many times expressed a

desire to see his farm so in 1857 James built an addition to his shanty home so that she might come and visit them. When she finally did come in August of that year she expressed delight over the place and had special praise for the iron cook stove that he had purchased from Paul Smith a couple of years earlier when he had come through from Vermont. She stayed until Christmas, cooking for the men, as well as helping James plan his new home building. James had just become involved in politics and was the first supervisor of the newly-formed Town of Brighton. In addition, he had just taken a contract for the building of a road across the big marsh to Bloomingdale . . . all of which provided money for the new house. He told the story that his guiding money paid for the furnishings.

After a bit he finally got started on the construction of his first real house, which was a two-story frame building with a living room and dining room on the first floor and six sleeping rooms on the second. The kitchen and woodshed joined to the dining room in an ell with bedrooms for the family over the kitchen area. The extra bedrooms were for the hunting and fishing parties that were discovering Wardner and his partners as fine guides. The three men were doing most of the work except some part-time help taking care of the house. In fact, this partnership continued for 15 years, ending in June, 1869, when Seth bought an adjoining farm and Lorenzo moved back to Keeseville.

The farm part of the project was producing pigs, cows, sheep, chickens, and bees. He first planted some corn for fodder but also had garden crops for use in the house and for winter.

When the house was completed and newly furnished he married Delia Marshall in June of 1860. Delia had been his childhood sweetheart and had waited all the years of his trip west, and all of the time spent regaining his health. After a trip to New York City, the couple came to Rainbow and she had her first look at the house he had built for her. A son Frank was born June 18, 1863. That summer, Addie Macomber, a former pupil of Delia's, came to help with the new baby.

Some years later Delia became ill, and died in 1871. After that, James married Addie who bore him another son, Charles, and two girls, Louise (Lula) and Katherine (Kit). Louise first married Herman Prellwitz and after his death, Fred Toof. They ran the Garondah for a while. Katherine married a man by the name of Tack and eventually moved out of the state.

On a stormy snowy day in February, 1873, fire broke out in a dirty chimney which spread to the entire house, leveling the building to the ground in no time. James and two hired men were away in the woods cutting cedar fence posts and Addie and a hired girl were at home alone when the fire broke out. The two women saved the baby, Louise, and quite a bit of the clothing, some dishes and food, by throwing things into the snow and later picking them up. They set up housekeeping in the barn for the rest of the winter, meanwhile making plans to clean up and rebuild in the spring.

The new place, which continued the fame of Rainbow Inn, was in a most desirable location with the lake before them and the lovely flower gardens around the finished building were a delight to the eye. The house was larger, but on the same general plan and with a third floor added.

Property owners in the upper end of the lake at the present time have James Wardner to thank for the good water in front of their camps. It was his dam at the lower end of the lake that raised the water level and joined three natural ponds into a solid waterway where one could travel for miles from any dock in Rainbow. He worked one whole winter hauling logs and large rocks at the best point at the lower end of the lake and when the ice melted in the spring his dam settled into place. It gave his property good deep frontage water and created many more feet of shoreland all around the upper end of the lake, where it had been sort of swampy.

In July, 1884, James Wardner became the first Postmaster of Rainbow, as the area was so named at the time. This was later renamed due to some confusion with a town in New Jersey. He held this post for many years. On the old postmark stamped on mail, not only was the date stamped but also Wardner's name and the town.

Another position James held was that of school commissioner for the county for a period of six years, 1882 to 1888. When the Town of Brighton was formed in 1858 he was already the Supervisor of Duane, so he automatically became Brighton's first Supervisor since he lived in our area. He served in this office for eight different years, the last time being in 1893.

In his later years he overextended his financial dealings and finally decided to sell the Inn property which was converted into the Rainbow Sanatorium. He died November 15, 1904.

SETH WARDNER, who was eight years older than his brother, James, was a surveyor. Much of the Brighton area was surveyed by him and his name appears on many old deeds.

APOLLOS A. SMITH. While Apollos Smith was not the first settler in the Town of Brighton, he certainly was one of the earliest. He came at a time when the area was ripe for development. Unquestionably, he was responsible for the influx of the many important people whose families came first as summer visitors and then stayed to become permanent residents, or returned each year to their lavish camps. It was his various business ventures that offered employment to all kinds of skills that attracted still others to settle in the area. Likewise, in the long run, it was the money he made that was used to start the college that continues to be the largest single factor in the growth of the Town of Brighton.

It was the patronage of people of wealth that enabled Paul Smith to expand a small sporting lodge into a million-dollar enterprise. His business ventures were not confined to running a hotel. There was a general store where all manner of supplies could be purchased. There was a sawmill to turn out the makings of the camps that were being built on the land that Paul sold to his wealthy summer visitors. There were motor-driven launches in his boathouse that made regular deliveries to the several lakes connected to his own Lower St. Regis Lake. His venture into electric power development brought electric lights to his community as early as 1894. By 1908 he had an electrically-operated train running between the Hotel and the New York Central station at Lake Clear, thus providing uninterrupted Pullman service from the hotel, east to New York, or west toward Chicago. Communication was important to his guests so he first ran a special stage to the nearest post office, and later, in 1881, he secured the first Post Office in the town. He was named Postmaster of the Paul Smiths Post Office, a position he held until his death. As the telephone and telegraph became important, he had this facility installed in his hotel as well as a stock exchange.

Apollos A. Smith, or Paul Smith as he was better known, was born in Milton, Vermont, on August 20, 1825. His father had lived in that area all his life, supporting his family by engaging in a lumber business, and at one time owned a grist mill as well as the sawmill. For many years he ran the Red Bird Stage Line that carried mail between Burlington and Montreal. Paul's mother was Marilla (Woodruff) Smith, whose family migrated from Connecticut to Vermont sometime around 1800. All that is known of them is that they were civic-minded and played a part in their town government. Paul was one of three children. There was a brother, Lewis, who was two years older, and a sister, Sarah, eleven years younger.

The name Appollos was a long one and it was soon shortened to "Pol" by those who knew him and that was how he later became known as Paul. He attended school in Vermont as a boy, but he always managed to find time for hunting, fishing and trapping. As far as can be determined, his school days did not last very long.

As a young man of 16, he and a friend began working on a merchant's line of boats that traveled from Lake Champlain to New York City. The boats going down had a cargo of grain and returned with a variety of merchandise and supplies that were dropped off along the landings on the Vermont shore, to be later transported inland. The trip would take two weeks and young Pol found it most exciting. Many times later he reflected that this was the nicest time of his life.

It was during this period of his life that Pol met a Captain Tucker who rewarded the boys with a trip into the Adirondacks, after the boats were put up for the winter. He brought them to the John Merrill place at Loon Lake. It was wild, rough country and no one had settled west of the Merrill place. Consequently, there was an abundance of game and fish to be found. This was much to Pol's liking and he made several trips to this area, staying at Merrill's. It was not long before he gained a reputation of knowing exactly where to find good catches of fish and game. It was a logical development that he was soon persuaded that he could use his natural ability as a sportsman to good advantage to earn

148

a living. All he needed was a sporting house of his own.

In 1848 he rented the old Lovering place (near where Ferd Chase later built Loon Lake House). He took it for three years and brought his mother and father along to help him. Pol did the guiding and his mother did the household chores. She was a fine cook and so between them they built a good reputation, very likely the basis for his future success. All the while he was renting, he kept looking for a place of his own and finally settled on 200 acres on the North Branch of the Saranac River, not far from the bridge on the Loon Lake road. This was the spot where he built his Hunter's Home, a simple wooden building with a kitchen and living room on the main floor and ten sleeping rooms on the top floor. It was far from fancy, but no women came to hunt, and the men were satisfied.

He finished Hunter's Home in 1852 and in April went to Grand Isle to get some furniture. His adventures on this trip he told in great detail many times in later years. He said that the ice was going out and he hired a man with a small pony to take him to Milton, which was on the other side of the Island. He got the furniture loaded on a sled and with his sister, Sarah, they headed for Grand Isle. He made Grand Isle all right, but the ice was breaking up fast and the man with the pony refused to go any further. Finally Paul put on the sled what things he could drag and Sarah and he started for Cumberland Head. Traveling got so bad he left Sarah on the ice and he went ashore to get some rope, so they could help each other as they jumped from one cake of ice to another. They finally made it to shore safely, but some of the furniture had to be brought from Grand Isle later.

The Hunter's Home venture lasted for six years with a considerable amount of success due in part to his guiding and the fine table he set. The customers were men of prominence and wealth, coming from Boston and New

York City. One such guest was Daniel Saunders, a well-known lawyer from Massachusetts. It was in the fall of 1858 that Paul brought the lawyer up into St. Regis Lake country on a trip. While eating their lunch that September day, they sat on a high bank overlooking Lower St. Regis Lake. Saunders was most impressed with the beautiful spot and suggested to Paul that this was where he should have his lodge. When they returned to Hunter's Home their conversation was retold to the group there and Dr. Hezekiah B. Loomis told Paul that he would back him with the building if Paul would buy the land. All this, providing Paul would build the new place large enough, and nice enough, so they could bring their wives on these hunting and fishing trips.

Paul was able to buy 50 acres at $6.00 an acre with what money he had. He borrowed $14,000 from Dr. Loomis to build the new house, which contained 17 bedrooms in addition to a large living room and the necessary kitchen and dining areas. The construction was started in December, 1858, and completed in the spring of 1859. He was all ready to open his new establishment except for one important detail, a personal matter that could not be overlooked.

This personal matter involved Lydia Helen Martin, born August 29, 1834, at Ausable Forks, one of eleven children of Hugh and Sarah (Goodell) Martin. Lydia received her education at the Emma Willard Seminary at Troy, N. Y. At this time few girls received this much education; this fact alone stamped her as an unusual young lady. Her education was classical in nature and included all the finer graces as well as considerable religious instruction. At the time Paul met Lydia, she was living with her family at Franklin Falls. They met at a dance near Loon Lake where Paul was established in his Hunter's Home. Lydia was an excellent dancer and especially loved the waltz, which was not well known in the area

150

at that time. Paul siezed this opportunity to gain her favor by quickly learning to do the waltz and so became her frequent partner at dances. He had eyes for no one else. The story is told that during the winter he was building on St. Regis, he traveled 20 miles on snowshoes to visit Lydia at Franklin Falls. He was 34 years old when they were married on May 5, 1859 (according to the marriage certificate found in the possessions of Phelps Smith, now in the Paul Smith's College Library collection).

It was a short honeymoon for the couple for their first guests at St. Regis began to arrive ten days later. Paul had left his father and mother to run Hunter's Home and he and Lydia began their lives as hotel-keepers on the spot that became known the world over as Paul Smith's, the fashionable hostelry of the Adirondacks. From the first Lydia proved to be a great asset to the business — personally supervising the thousand-and-one details of cooking and cleaning. She managed so well that each guest had nothing but praise for the establishment. Paul was quick to realize this, and pleased too, for this left him free to be the jovial host and guide.

Paul was a lanky man, slightly stooped and lame in his later years, but his keen sense of humor, alert mind, and fondness for jokes made him a popular host all during his lifetime. He was shrewd and deadly serious when involved in a business deal, but had an eternal well of optimism about the future and to the end of his time seemed to have a continual drive pushing him into all manner of ventures to earn money. Like all Adirondack guides, his first love seemed to be telling stories to entertain the "city folks" and he wasn't adverse to playing practical jokes on them either.

One author spoke of him as being "apathetic and indolent in temperament." Yet his passive nature could be, and often was, aroused when something did not meet

151

with his approval. Paul was very strong, as demonstrated by the time he and his brother-in-law, Charlie Martin, raised a heavy supporting post for an addition to the hotel. This is one of the times he was aroused, for this was done to demonstrate to his boss mechanic that all the men the boss had requested were unnecessary for such a simple job.

His keen sense of humor made him the center of any group and the fund of his stories seemed limitless as over the years I heard a great variety of them retold by the local folks who remembered Paul Smith.

There was a great joy on March 4, 1861, when the first child born to Paul and Lydia was a son. They named him Henry B. L. Smith, after Dr. Loomis who had backed Paul financially in his St. Regis Hotel. Henry, according to what records are available, was a great favorite of his mother. School attendance records for the town on file in the Town Hall include Easy Street School from 1871 on, but do not show any record of Henry attending this school. However, it has been determined that Henry, as a child, was a part of a small class of youngsters that were taught during the winter months by Charles Martin (Lydia's brother) in the Smith home.

On June 4, 1862, the second son was born. He was named Phelps, after Paul's father. School attendance records show that Phelps attended the Easy Street School in 1874 and 1875. There were several years missing in the records at this time so it is not certain they did get the rest of their elementary education. After Paul purchased their Fouquet House in 1875 the family began to spend winters there for several years. So it is possible that the boys attended school in Plattsburgh some of the time. Phelps was a graduate of Eastman Business College at Poughkeepsie in the class of May 11, 1881, according to his diploma. A letter found in his possessions, after his death, indicated that his teachers highly recommended him at the time of his graduation.

A third son, Apollos A. Smith, Jr., was born nine years later on August 3, 1871. School records show that Paulie, as he became popularly known, attended Brighton District No. 1 during the years 1880 to 1882, and in the summer of 1885. However, it seems likely that most of his education was gained at Trinity School at Peekskill, (a very strict Military Academy). One of Lydia's letters dated June 8, 1886, written to Phelps at Plattsburgh, spoke of Paulie being away at school for two years and no one having gone to visit him. She suggested that Phelps accompany her on such a visit in hopes of encouraging better work from Paulie. Later in 1888, Paulie wrote of liking school; then in March, 1889, Lydia received a report from the school that Paulie's work was extremely good and that he had been promoted to Lieutenant. He had been to New York and got his new uniform. It cost $80 and he was right proud of it. Another of Lydia's letters told of sending him money for boxing, dancing, and banjo lessons with the wish that he would improve himself all he could. In a yearbook of the school it was recorded that Paulie won the prize for Very Great Improvement. He was a member of the telegraph club, a roller skating club, and rowed in place four in his boat club.

One thing for sure — all of the boys received more than the usual schooling, very likely because of their mother's interest in education. Paul, Sr., had very little respect for education, for he felt that a person was born with what ability he had and all the schooling in the world could not alter that native ability.

When their little hotel opened, the Civil War was almost upon the nation, and when the war came it gave extra impetus to their business. The hotel was filled with men of wealth who could afford to hire someone to go to

153

war in their place. At the close of the war, the hotel was all paid for with $50,000 to the good; their happy home had children; the business was growing rapidly, and the combined efforts of Paul and Lydia seemed destined for success.

Paul continued to acquire land, some costing him as little as $1.50 an acre. He bought this land all around his original 50 acres until he had nearly 30,000 acres, including ten lakes which he owned in their entirety. He never kept the public from using his lakes for fishing and boating and his woodlands were always available to the hunter. This policy is mostly continued today, for few of the more than 20,000 acres still owned by the College display any posted signs. The story is recorded that in 1903 when forest fires raged over a nearby forest preserve, the local people refused to help, although they were offered $4 a day. However, they were always ready and willing to help Uncle Paul fight his fires, for Paul let them use his land while the owner of the private preserve would not.

Sometime before 1875 they expanded their hotel business with the purchase of the Fouquet House in Plattsburgh, located right across from the railroad station. They ran it themselves for a few years during the winter months, leaving the St. Regis Hotel to a winter caretaker. By 1885 Phelps was through school and Lydia's letters to him indicate that he was managing the Fouquet House

Paul and Lydia began to take winter trips to Florida, and her letters refer to her "cough" that seemed to be a source of concern to them both. When Phelps took a trip to Denver, Colorado, sometime in 1887, Dr. Loomis advised her against going because of her weak throat and lungs. She did not go.

By 1890 the three boys were grown up and had already assumed some of the family responsibilities of the

154

hotel business, so, on December 12th that year, Paul, Lydia and the boys organized the Paul Smith's Hotel Company. From then until 1905 the company grew and developed by leaps and bounds. They greatly enlarged the hotel; built a new store, some dormitories for the help, several shops, a four-story warehouse, a stable for 60 fine horses, laundry, wood sheds, sawmills, and winter living quarters for the family that also was large enough to provide much needed office space. It was during this expansion that the first casino was put on the lake shore as well as a new boathouse.

With all this success it would seem that the Smith family would be a happy one, but that was not exactly the case. As the boys were growing up, some friction developed between the brothers, Henry and Phelps. Henry semed to prefer the company of the guides and tried to be like them in manner, dress, and speech. He also developed a fondness for drink. In direct contrast, Phelps was all business, serious and most careful of his appearance. This friction was a great worry to their mother and father, and each in his own way tried to bring about a better relationship between the boys, without much success. In her letters, Lydia showed that she was troubled about Henry's behavior, for she dearly loved her firstborn.

Lydia and Paul were on their way south in 1891 when word reached them of Henry's death on January 3rd, apparently from pneumonia. This was a great blow to them, and they took their loss with many a tear shed in the privacy of their room. Almost daily a letter was written to Phelps and Paulie that winter, as they once again started south — each one filled with their grief. Later Lydia wrote in Henry's prayer book her outpouring of this grief: "My precious child is gone and Mother's heart is full of sorrow." As 1891 progressed, she continued to write in his book — in February, in April, in June and

155

July — asking *why* God had taken Henry and where she had failed.

While Lydia's letter in 1891 seemed to indicate her general good health, she did mention that Paul was not too well. They were still mourning over Henry's death. In her last letter written to her sister, Lucy, dated November 2nd, she wrote: "I put on my big felt shoes this morning as my feet are cold. We are all quite well. Grandma (Paul's mother, then 91 years old) cried all morning for her boy who is gone . . . " In spite of her "quite well" statement, she died three days later on November 5th. Many felt she grieved so much over Henry's death that she had no more fighting spirit to overcome her own physical illness.

Old Paul, at 66, had lost his waltzing Lydia. These two deaths in one year were hard medicine for the old man, but his common sense made him realize that keeping busy would help ease his heartache. He had the two boys, Phelps and Paulie, and he literally dove into the big expansion program they had planned for the newly-formed company. Few people realized how deeply Paul felt about his losses, for his Yankee pride kept his sorrow private as he presented his best, jovial self to friends and neighbors. But the two boys knew and tried to help him all they could.

Paul began traveling more than he had in the past, visiting nearly all the important cities and resorts in the United States and Canada. Gradually the two sons assumed more and more of the responsibilities of the Smith enterprise.

A reporter interview him in the spring of 1910 about his health and Paul stated his feeling about the whole deal. He declared that fresh air should be taken in moderation. "Medicine ruins your stomach. It's nasty stuff. If I must have a doctor, give me one that don't give any medicine." He had been having a little trouble with his heart and he was not well all that summer. He stated that he would never take "Beruna or Bluffy's Malt." His favorite prescription was bread and milk, at that time.

Books and education were regarded by Paul as "frills." He once remarked, "No fool like an educated one" to Dr. Trudeau, after being told by a learned man how he ought to run his hotel. Paul delighted in proving that, even with his little schooling, he was more than a match for all the educated shrewdness that crossed his path.

Popularity and success never seemed to change Paul. To the very end of his life, he remained simple and unaffected . . . always himself. He drank and smoked, but never to excess. He was always one to retire early and was up early and ready for what the day would bring. The only really serious illness that afflicted him was the last one.

Paul had to have a kidney removed in October, 1912. He was in the Royal Victoria Hospital in Montreal and getting along in his recovery perfectly. However, several weeks later another operation became necessary and Paul did not recover from this one. It was on December 15, 1912, at this same hospital that the grand old man of the Adirondacks found himself at his final destination. At the age of eighty-seven, his death made headlines around the world. Hundreds of messages of condolence poured in and hundreds came for the funeral service held in St. John's in the Wilderness. He is buried in the cemetery adjacent to the church.

And so old Paul was gone. Gone but not forgotten, for each man leaves his mark on the place where he lived — leaving some evidence of how he lived. Paul Smith did that in many ways. He had made friends of the people who worked for him, and just as easily made friends with Presidents, like Grover Cleveland, Harrison, and Teddy Roosevelt He had charmed a wide variety of other folks from P. T. Barnum to Dr. Trudeau and E. H. Harriman, the railroad king. So when he died the testimony of hundreds paid him homage in writing and in person.

After Paul's death the two sons carried on the business. Both had enough education and inherited ability to do this. Paul, Jr., realizing that he was in failing health, sold his interest in 1925, and he died in 1927. Phelps continued to run the company until his death in 1937. Phelps had never married, and in his will he directed that his wealth and property be used to establish a co-educational non-sectarian college at Paul Smiths, to be known as Paul Smith's College, in memory of his father.

From the Town of Brighton records, as well as letters and papers of the Smith family, their contributions to the community are found to be numerous. Apollos was Supervisor of the town in 1863, and again from 1866 to 1875. Henry, the oldest son, held the same office from 1884 until his death in January of 1891. Then Phelps took over and he was re-elected in 1892. The present Town Hall and Garage are located on land donated by Phelps in 1914. The first church in the area, St. John's in the Wilderness, was made of logs given by Paul in 1877 and built on land given by him. Lydia was responsible for the Methodist Church, built between Paul Smiths and Gabriels, now made over into a faculty residence. She raised money for its construction on Smith land. Land was donated for both the local Catholic Church and Keeses Mill Presbyterian Church. When the Sisters of Mercy found it difficult to find money for the purchase of land for their proposed sanatorium, Paul and his friend, Dr. W. S. Webb (N. Y. Central Railroad) each presented the Sisters with 50 acres of land in Gabriels. Lydia was constantly making generous contributions of money to all area churches. Few people know that Paul Smith's Hotel Company gave the land for the present Saranac Lake Airport. The College created by Phelps'

158

will has been a profound influence on the Town of Brighton, financially and otherwise, and this Smith influence will continue well into the forseeable future.

FRANK ALEXANDER was probably the only inventor in the town who actually patented his product. The local papers carried the news story in December, 1909. "The Adirondack Snow Packer & Track Cleaner, patented in the United States & Canada by Alexander-Muncil Co., is being welcomed by all northern New Yorkers who travel afoot or by sleigh. This device was invented by Frank Alexander of Paul Smiths and is a decided improvement over all previous snow road builders."

ORMAN DOTY was born over in Vermontville, on Pigeon Hill, May 7, 1882. His father had a farm on this hardwood hill back up at the foot of Kate Mt. When Orman was a few years old the family moved to Brighton, about a quarter of a mile from where the Town Hall is now. The house was on the left hand side of the road coming toward Rainbow. The family home burned when Orman was nine and the woods caught fire, burning all the way to where Meagher's Mill is now. In telling about the fire, Orman said, "They didn't really fight fire then. Folks didn't have anything to fight with. There were three houses there, but a gang of men saved the other two houses. Then we moved to a log house about where the Town Hall is now."

Orman was one of the pupils in the school at the top of Easy Street hill, across from Phil King's place. He was about ten years old when the following incident took place.

"They come there, goin' around vaccinating all the children for small pox. Well, as I sat at my desk, there

159

was a window there, and it was about half way open. This big old Doctor came in. I remember him well. His name was Dr Church, and he got this girl and he scratched her arm She screamed! *Swish* (and he clapped his hands to illustrate)and I was out the window, and he out the door after me. I took right down across the field and into the woods.

"He came down to see my Dad and said, "You'll have to bring that boy down. He'll have to be vaccinated. Gosh darn little cuss can run like a rabbit.

"I didn't go down and I was never vaccinated until I was 31 years old working in a box factory in New Hampshire. One day they took out five with small pox and they came through vaccinating. I was sicker than anyone who had the pox. Thought for a while I would lose my arm."

From 1914 until his death, Orman lived at Rainbow. He and his wife, Theresa, had two children, Alvin and Thelma. The Dotys operated the Rainbow Lake Cottage, which took summer boarders and hunters. Their "people" came back year after year for the fine meals and to hear Orman's stories.

Orman was a registered guide, had excellent eyesight, and could find his way in any woods, no matter how remote. These were some of the reasons, plus the fact that he did not drink, why he was selected to be Calvin Coolidge's guide when the President spent the summer here at White Pine Camp, in 1926.

In speaking of the President, Orman said, "He was a quiet man. Never spoke a cross word; never hummed a tune; never mentioned politics."

Early in his guiding work, Orman had learned that he must keep his parties entertained. One time he was desperate for a story when he and the President were out fishing. After it had been quiet for quite a while he came up with this one:

"I was in a boat washing a red flannel shirt and a big

160

pike came up and swallowed everything but the sleeve I had a hold of. The pike started off and I hung on, because it was my best shirt. When I finally got scared and let go, the boat was going so fast that it ran 20 feet on shore and smashed to splinters."

"Is that so," said Coolidge, and never cracked a smile.

"So," Orman said, "I tried another about the time I caught four fish on one hook. You see a sucker swallowed a worm, and then a trout swallowed the sucker, then a bass came along and grabbed the trout, and finally a good big pike gobbled the bass."

"That's very interesting," said the President, and went on fishing.

Orman had just happened to mention earlier about a 19-pounder pike that he had caught earlier in the season. He could tell Coolidge didn't believe a word of it, but the President didn't say so. A bit later that afternoon, Orman pulled out one that went 18 pounds.

The President began to laugh. "Apologies, Doty. I'll believe everything you tell me after this."

After this summer of 1926, Orman became somewhat of a celebrity because of his guiding for Coolidge. He had always had a good business, but after all the publicity, he became more and more in demand as a guide.

He was active and alert in mind until his death in 1972, in his 90th year. Mrs. Doty died in December, 1973. The son, Alvin, still lives in Rainbow Lake and their daughter, Mrs. Thelma Caswell, lives in Florida.

JAMES PRELLWITZ, grandson of James Wardner, was born at Rainbow Lake in October, 1895, and still lives in the area. He did some guiding and was a camp caretaker for many years before his retirement. He and his wife, Flo Bryant, brought up their family on the island "hogback" in Rainbow Lake. During the late fall, before the ice was thick enough to walk on, Jim had to keep a narrow channel free of ice, to push his boat through in order to get to the mainland. This was done daily so that his son Herman and daughter Jean might get to school. The process was repeated in the spring when the ice became too dangerous to use. There were times when it was necessary for Jim to walk the length of the "hogback" and around the end of the lake in order to get out to the road and thus get necessary supplies.

CHARLES RILEY was born in Bangor, September 27, 1876, and educated in the public schools of Bangor and Brushton. He worked for his father on their farm for a short time and at the age of 22 came to Gabriels to work for Barney Lantry in his general store. In 1900 he purchased the Zeb Robare property that was a small hotel. In 1918 he enlarged and remodeled it, calling it the Riley Hotel. He was married to Mary E. Brown of Malone in November, 1903, and they had three children — William E, now living in Gabriels; Mary and Charles J. Mr. Riley was a Democrat and took a keen interest in politics. He served as a Town Supervisor, 1909-1923, and 1934-1935. Prior to becoming Supervisor he was Town Assessor from 1903-1907.

CHARLES WARDNER was born at Rainbow Lake in 1878, the son of James M. and Addie Macomber Wardner. For 51 years he operated the Clark-Wardner Camps (16 cottages and main lodge) on Rainbow Lake, previous to his retirement in 1952. He was a school teacher during the regular part of the year and looked after the camps in the summer. He was a born story-teller and authored "Footprints on Adirondack Trails" in manuscript form.

162

A son, Walter Wardner, still spends the summer at the camp, together with his family.

DR. J. SEYMOUR EMANS came to the area as Resident Physician of the Foresters Sanatorium at Rainbow. He had been living at Gabriels since 1908 and moved to Rainbow when the San opened in 1910. He served as Town Health Officer after 1916, and was also school doctor and the one first called in any local emergency. In 1925 he retired from the San and died on March 14, 1936.

AMIEL G. McCOLLOM, who was for many years known as "Uncle Mac," was born in 1819. About 1874 he was working for the builders of the Ogdensburgh railroad and his contacts on the job gave him the idea that some "burnt land" was available, so he investigated. Burnt land was just what the name suggested . . . land ravaged by forest fires. The site pleased him and he moved his family into their new home, a large log structure that had been built earlier by Amos Rice, an earlier settler in the north end of the town. At first he just farmed it mostly; hunting and fishing just for himself. Then, since his reputation as a good sportsman spread, and since the house was larger than his family needed, he began to take in hunters and fishermen. So he probably was the first hotel-keeper in the town. It was hard work to keep the family going so he tried a sideline of growing hops. That did not turn out very well, but a second sideline of a milk route down to the wealthy camps on the St. Regis Lakes was much more successful. Things never did go well for him as far as the family was concerned, as his children, five in number, all died young of an epidemic that swept the area. His wife died in 1890 and he followed soon in 1893 at the age of 74. All of them are buried in the burying ground next to the McCollom's house. This is now one of the official town cemeteries in Brighton.

EARL C. McARTHUR was born July 15, 1888, at Mc-Colloms, son of Clarence A. McArthur and Cecile V. Hutchins. His early education was in McCollom's school and he went on to high school in Malone, graduating from Franklin Academy. He attended Yale University where he attracted considerable fame as a football player. After his graduation from Yale in 1910 he distinguished himself as an English teacher at Peddy Institute at Hightstown, New Jersey. For several years he was in charge of that school's summer camp on Osgood Pond. He was a natural selection for this job as he knew and loved the woods, having grown up in the area and been associated with this type of life with his father. He retired from Peddy in 1936 to assume the position of the first President of the newly-formed Paul Smith's College. This was a most difficult job as he was responsible for the planning of a collegiate institution, taking into consideration the terms of the will of Phelps Smith, requirements of the Charter and the Board of Regents, as well as the physical and financial means available. He was a logical choice for this position as he was not only a local boy but a member of the original incorporating Trustees of the College. During the time he was President, many litigations over the will and World War II prevented an official opening of the College. However, during his tenure the campus was used for training a WAC Contingent and to base the Signal Corps training school. He resigned as President in December of 1945 after serious philosophical differences between himself and the Board could not be resolved. After this he left the area and assumed new duties as Associate Professor of English with Associated Colleges of Upper New York at Mohawk College

164

in Utica. From there he went to the expanding state college system at Plattsburgh and later at Penn Yan. In 1955 he sold the family home at McColloms and was only an occasional visitor after that. His health declined rapidly in these years and he died on May 24, 1965, at Penn Yan, a few days after making the trip to McColloms to bury his sister, Gladys. He is also buried at the family plot at McColloms. He was married to Eleanor Hammell of New Jersey and had two daughters.

SISTER M. PERPETUAL HELP KIERAN was born in Omagh, Ireland, October 8, 1845. Her education was begun in her native town and completed at the Convent in York, England. Sister came to Canada about 1870 and was one of three original postulants to join the ranks of the Sisters of Mercy at Malone on January 1, 1875. For forty-one years she devoted herself to the work of her Order with great energy and steadfastness. After months of discouraging attempts to start the Sanatorium they desired, she and her co-worker, Sister M. McAuley, found friends who donated money, and Dr. Webb and Paul Smith, who gave the land, and with these gifts they started Gabriels San. The story of her life is the history of the Sanatorium she worked so diligently to build. Sister died at Gabriels on July 24, 1914, and is buried in the Sisters' cemetery.

BENJAMIN ARTHUR MUNCIL was born August 28, 1876, in the Town of Franklin but almost his entire life was spent in Brighton. He was the sixth child in a family of nine children. When he was five, his mother died and his father, unable to care for these small children, placed them in different homes. His education was very limited because of this, for he was forced to work so much of the

165

time when he should have been in school. In his early teens he began to work in the woods, lumbering in the winter and then in the summer he worked at Paul Smith's Hotel. He also worked as a guide for the campers on the St. Regis Lakes. He was twenty-three when he married Mary Elizabeth Quaine of Bombay. He became interested in sawmilling and the building business but realized he needed more education to do this. With the help of his wife he studied and read at home. The big dream of his life was to build fine camps that he could envision but he could not put them on paper. Consequently, he took a correspondence course in architecture and learned to reduce his ideas to plans on paper. He owned a sawmill and contracting business from about 1893 on and was responsible for building many of the fine camps on the lakes. He expanded his mill operation to Gabriels in 1913 but most of his business was centered around his home area on the Keeses Mill Road near Paul Smiths. His business was incorporated in 1929 as B. A. Muncil & son with his son, B. A. Muncil, Jr., as vice-president, and son-in-law, Cornelius Meagher, as secretary-treasurer. One of his well-known pieces of construction was at the Post Camp on Upper St. Regis Lake. In addition to his contracting business, he was also Town Superintendent of Highways for several years. On December 16, 1930, he was killed at the Gabriels railroad crossing. In addition to B. A. Muncil, Jr., he had one daughter, Leah Mary, who was married to C. F. Meagher.

FRED MARTIN settled on his farm in Gabriels about 1893. He was the brother-in-law of Apollos Smith and guided at the hotel as well as farmed on the side. It was his son, Douglas, that took over this farm in 1927. At first he had dairy cows but soon joined the other big farmers in the area in growing certified seed potatoes.

166

When Douglas died in 1958 he had no sons to continue the business and the farm was sold to David Young from Long Island in 1960.

BENJAMIN F. HOBART bought his first farm in the Brighton area in the 1870's. He had come first to Keeses Mills to work in the lumber mill started there, but after that operation closed down he stayed to farm it and to act as caretaker for the Penfold family who had a summer camp on Upper St. Regis Lake. In the meantime he had established a farm site in the Gabriels area. His son, Henry (married to Milly Doty, Orman Doty's sister) took over the caretaker job and the farm. A son was born to them in 1892 whom they named Frank.

FRANK HOBART took over his father's farm and continued to build up his reputation as a grower of certified seed potato seed along with the Leavitt's and Martin's. He increased the size of the farm until it was considered to be a big farm for the times and the area. For a while he grew a considerable amount of truck vegetables which were shipped to the New York market, but his main crop was potatoes. He was married first to Stella Downs who died in 1947; and later to Kathryn Daly who died in 1965. Frank passed away in 1966 and the farm is now owned by Mark and Don Tucker who continue the potato business.

ARTHUR LEAVITT came to Gabriels when he was six years old with his father, Lyman, and his mother, Ada Jenkins Leavitt. Arthur had been born in Bloomingdale October 16, 1884. When the family first came they bought land of Guy Rand and farmed it some but his

167

father also lumbered quite a bit. On the farm they grew just about everything for their own needs and there was a cow or two and a team of horses. The family consisted of three children, Arthur, Charles and Mabel. The original homestead was where Mabel lives now, but the first house burned and the present house is a new one. Their neighbors were Guy Rand (Young farm) and Zeb Robare (where Leavitt home is now). The school that Arthur attended was where Charlie Martin lives now. One of Arthur's early memories was when the first train came through Gabriels. It was quite an event. Arthur lived to see the last train go by and to see the removal of the tracks. Leavitt's always grew table potatoes and after Arthur completed a short course in agriculture at Cornell he became the farm manager in 1912. It was about this time that he began to develop a good seed potato business, selling to Long Island farmers. In the early 1920's Mr. Leavitt, joined by two other growers in Gabriels, Frank Hobart and Douglas Martin, formed the Northern N.Y. Seed Growers Association with their own inspector. Gradually he increased his acreage, buying up some of his grandfather Jenkins' farm and the Zeb Robare farm, then owned by Moses Russell, Zeb's son-in-law. Arthur was married to Eleanor McMaster and they had a son, William, and a daughter, Eleanor. William Leavitt and his sons continue to operate the large potato farm.

RICHARD J. LONGTIN, who was born in Bennington, Vermont, on Sept. 27, 1888, came to work for the Paul Smiths' Hotel as a young man of 20 years. He worked in the office and spent his entire life working for the family in the various Smith enterprises. Only during World War I (from May 27, 1918, to July 9, 1919) did he leave the area while he served as a sergeant in Company B, Second Pioneer Infantry in France. After old Paul Smith died, Mr. Longtin became more and more useful to Phelps in the operation of the business and when Phelps died in 1937 it was Longtin who took over the operation of the Power & Light Co., and the Hotel Co. For 25 years he was Postmaster of Paul Smiths and he also served as Town Supervisor from 1924 to 1933. During his entire life he was active in all community affairs until his retirement because of poor health shortly after 1962. Mr. Longtin had been living in the Smith Hotel and escaped from the building when it burned in 1962, but he suffered a severe personal loss of historical possessions collected over the years, in addition to smoke inhalation. The combination seemed to rob him of all inclination to live. His decline was steady from then until his death on July 29, 1967.

Old Time Tales

Sylvester "Ves" Otis as a young lad had lived on Barnum Pond in a cabin. He showed a real knack for guiding and often came to the Cranford Camp to guide. Soon after the Civil War broke out, he ran away and joined up as a drummer boy. However, they soon found out that he was a better scout than a drummer. One day he spotted a northern lieutenant with a group of spies to be shot. He trailed them for a time and at one point the group had to cross a fence. In doing so, one of the "spies" tore his trousers and much to Ves' surprise he noted that the leg so exposed was that of a woman. He circled around the area and came back to face the group, and spoke to the lieutenant.

169

"You wouldn't shoot a woman, would you?" Ves asked.

"No," came the reply.

Ves was hard put to explain, for in those days a woman's leg was a delicate subject. Finally he faced the problem squarely and explained to the officer that when the group had crossed the fence he had seen the leg, and that it was not the leg of a man.

Upon investigation the officer was convinced that one of his "spies" was a young woman dressed in men's clothing, and so spared her life.

Years later at the Paul Smiths' Hotel boathouse a woman standing on the docks heard someone call "Ves." She approached him and asked, "Are you "Ves" Sylvester Otis?"

Yes, Mam."

"Have you ever seen me before,"

"No mam."

"Look again."

"No mam."

"Well I was the girl you saved from being shot as a spy."

(as told by Margaret Cranford)

Caught in a Bear Trap

The Adirondack Mountains were but little known until after the American soldiers built the now famous "Northwest Bay Road" during the War of 1812. This road was built through trackless forests from Northwest Bay on Lake Champlain for the purpose of intercepting the British on the St. Lawrence River when navigation should open the next spring. Over this road traveled all of the early pioneers to the North Woods, as the great Adirondack wilderness was called by people in the central part of the state. Among these early pioneers were

170

three young men who had formed a co-partnership for the purpose of trapping and hunting furs for market. The North Woods were then filled with fur-bearing animals and game of all kinds. The trappers in those days got a much higher price for their furs than they can get at the present time, even though many of the fur-bearing animals are now almost extinct.

These three young men, Seth and James Wardner and Lorenzo Rand, in the summer of 1854, followed the old military road. With their camping outfit and canoe loaded on an old-fashioned buckboard wagon drawn by one horse, they took life easy and went as they pleased. Starting as they did, early in June, there was no need to hurry. They had all summer before them in which to choose a good camping place and get located before the autumn hunting and trapping would begin.

Many and exciting were their experiences on that trip, but at last after weeks of travel they selected a location for their camp on the west shore of what is now called Osgood Lake. Here they made a small clearing and built a shanty. Finding that the hunting was much better on the tributaries of the Saranac River system, they soon left their shanty on Osgood Lake and built another log cabin on the site which was afterwards occupied by the once-famous Rainbow Lake Inn.

Here in their snug little cabin, the two brothers and their friend, who was almost a brother to them, lived and continued their partnership for fifteen years. Each had his particular part of the housework to do. On Seth fell the duty of mending their clothes and knitting woolen socks and mittens. During the long winter evenings while James, the bookkeeper, wrote his daily accounts of the hunting and trapping, and Lorenzo molded lead bullets, or strung snowshoes, Seth would sit and click his knitting needles by the light of the open fire.

During the latter part of August each year the partners would begin to put out their line of sable and bear traps, which they visited once a week. James owned one monstrous bear trap having four extra heavy springs. The massive jaws armed with sharp steel spikes, looked, when opened, like the mouth of a huge shark. It was considered the work of two men to set this trap, but James, who was a powerful young man, had on several occasions succeeded in setting it by the aid of levers weighted down with a log.

That spring the partners had cleared quite a piece of land and had planted it to corn and rye. The grain was now ripe and suffering to be harvested, and as all the bear traps were set the partners began gathering in their crops.

One morning James had a severe attack of "chills and fever" as he had not yet gotten the malaria out of his system which he had contracted while living in Ohio.

"Well, Jim, you look like the last rose o'summer sitting there by the fire a shivering this hot day," said Seth as he came in to breakfast and found James with his overcoat on, humped over the fire shaking with the chills.

"I recon you had better stay inside today. Ren and I can finish up the grain all right, then we can all go look at the traps tomorrow. When you cool off from the fever you'll have after this chill you might finish oiling those deer hides we're tanning."

By afternoon James was feeling himself again. After doing up all the odd jobs around the cabin he took his gun and started out to look at some of the traps and shoot a few partridges for supper. After a half-hour tramp through the woods without seeing any partridge, he came to the big bear trap which they had set in an angle formed by two tree trunks. One of the tree trunks forming the angle lay across the other and up from the ground. The space between the log and the ground had been filled

172

with sticks and limbs, thus forcing the bear to approach over the trap in order to reach the bait placed in the corner.

A short, heavy chain attached the trap to a "clog" formed by a small log six inches in diameter and about 12 feet long. The trap was then neatly buried in the moss.

On approaching the trap, James found that it was sprung but contained only a porcupine. In their haste in first setting the trap they had forgotten to put the bent stick under the trigger which would prevent any light animal from springing the trap.

"Well, muttered James to himself, "there's one fool hedgehog less in the woods anyway." Then glancing up at the sun now sinking into the west, "I'll have to hustle and reset this trap if I get back to camp before dark."

Leaning his gun up against a tree, he pulled of his coat and began the task of resetting the big trap. Placing one end of a long lever under the bottom log on one side of the angle, he pressed down the two large springs at one end of the trap and placed a small log on the end of the lever to hold it down. Then taking another lever he pressed down the springs at the other end of the trap and, as no log was at hand to hold the other end, he thrust this end of the lever under a projecting root of a tree. Spreading the jaws of the trap apart he held them down with a foot on each while he reached down to pull up the trigger pan. Just as he did so the log on one end of the first lever rolled off and struck the root holding the other lever, thus releasing all of the springs at once. The four hundred pounds pressure of the steel springs brought the ugly spike-armed jaws together. So quickly was it done that James had no time to get out of the way. His right hand and the toes of both feet were held fast in the trap. A spike had passed through the toe of each of his cowhide boots, and another spike had passed through the flesh of his hand between the second and third finger. In this cramped position James rolled over on his side and lay for some time studying on how he might escape. It was useless to shout for help or to think of being found in time by the others as they did not know that he had gone to the traps. After struggling for a time, he lay still again, almost exhausted.

A stealthy noise in the leaves nearby sent the cold chills down his back. He knew what it was. A wolf slowly raised its head over the log and sniffed the air. Grabbing a handful of dead leaves he threw them at the wolf and shouted with all his might. The animal was evidently alone as it ran back a short distance, then sat down and began to howl. Knowing that this meant a call to the pack, James renewed his efforts to escape. His gun was entirely out of reach and his Navy revolver was in his belt on his right side just where he could not get it with his free left hand. Struggling frantically he tried to tear the flesh of his hand and so free his right hand, but the spike had passed through behind a cord. Then, by prying on the jaws with a stick in his left hand, he succeeded in pulling first one foot and then the other out of his cow-hide boots. In doing so it tore the end out of his socks and took the skin off several toes. Then with his feet free he worked himself over until he got his knees on the springs and his shoulders under the upper log. With an almost super-human effort he succeeded in bending the springs sufficiently to release his hand and his boots. Then, with the perspiration streaming off his face, he hurried back to camp, and just in time too; as he stumbled along through the now dark forest, the howling of the wolf pack told him of the fate he had barely escaped. Needless to say, James never tried to set the big bear trap alone after that.

(as recorded by Charles Wardner from the
stories told by his father, James Wardner)

174

An undated letter to the editor written by E. Long gives some interesting facts about pike and pickerel. He claims that the first of these fish to come to Osgood were caught through the ice in the Saranac River between Franklin Falls and Bloomingdale. Two farmers and two guides transferred two live pickerel to Osgood through a hole in the ice. This was about 1882. The two farmers were Phil King and his brother-in-law, Zeb Robare. These farmers both lived in the Town of Brighton. One of the guides was Jim Cross, who was six feet four inches tall and wore a long black beard. He also lived in Brighton, three miles below Paul Smiths, on the road to Buck Mountain. The other guide was Jim Bruce of Bloomingdale.

Mr. Long said that he lived in Brighton in the early eighties in a log house that commanded a view of Jones Pond nearby, and a good part of Osgood that is about a mile and half below Jones.

Paul Smith had friends from all walks of life, from the Indians who camped near the present college gym, selling their wares to the summer people, to the well-known statesmen who came to his hotel. When Grover Cleveland was Governor of New York he once spent a month with Paul, camping and fishing in the mountain lakes. Cleveland became well acquainted with Paul and one day turned to Paul and asked, "Paul, what can I do for you,"

Smith replied, "Governor, you've got nothing you can give me except your friendship."

The Governor, used to everyone wanting something, replied, "Paul, that is the most friendly act I have ever received."

P. T. Barnum visited Smith's often and Paul named Barnum Pond after him. Henry Firestone, who had a summer camp nearby, and E. H. Harriman were also close friends.

———————

Many political stories have been told about Paul Smith, but this was a new one that I found in a newspaper clipping. This caucus took place in the eighties, probably 1888, and was held at the King place for the purpose of nominating a ticket to be elected at the coming town meeting. At this time there were two political factions; Smith's was one and the other was the Wardner group, so a hot meeting was expected with each side anxious to get certain members of its own party on the slate.

The Smith group decided to spring a snap caucus, getting to the meeting ahead of the others, nominate their ticket, and adjourn. They carried it out accordingly. They arrived early and as they marched into the building with Charlie Martin in the lead, Charlie called out:

"Paul, will you be chairman?" Paul said "Yes" and it was voted unanimously before they were even seated.

Paul said to Henry Smith, "Will you be secretary and clerk?" "Yep," said Henry.

"Charlie Martin, will you be supervisor?" asked Paul. "Yes," answered Charlie.

"Be sure you get all this set down, Henry," said Paul. "Boys, I think I had better be assessor, and will you be collector, Henry?" "Yes," said Henry.

And so they went through the entire ticket in a hurry and, as they finished up, the crowd called for a few remarks from the chairman. Paul rose and said:

"I am not used to public speaking; but, boys, this is a damned good ticket and I don't see why it can't be elected. Let's adjourn before the other crew gets here."

———————

During 1926 President and Mrs. Calvin Coolidge spent the summer at White Pine Camp. That year as they circled Osgood in their boat, they had many fine places to look at. They would pass the exclusive camp conducted by William Root. The young son of the late Colonel John Jacob Astor, by his second wife, was camping there. Next was the camp of D. Douglas Franchot, of Oklahoma, who had three children with them. Beyond was the camp of Mrs. Gideon Lee's two daughters, Mrs. J. M. Cooper and Mrs. George Colvocarres. Next was the magnificent camp of Dr. Wilford McDougall. It cost $300,000, nearly as much as White Pine occupied by the Coolidge family. Then comes the woodsy type buildings that make up the Drexel Godfrey camp. On an island is the J. B. Cranford camp and not far away is the educational girls' camp conducted by Miss Lisle of Boston.

One of the cottages at Paul Smith's Hotel was made into the executive offices of the summer White House with Everett Sanders, secretary to the President, in charge. Another cottage became the telegraph office equipped to send news by the dozen expert operators present to handle the instruments.

It was July seventh when the special train carrying the President and Mrs. Coolidge arrived at Gabriels at 9:53 A.M. They left their private car, acknowledging the greetings of the local people who had gathered to greet them and then were driven to White Pine, six miles away.

The Marine Guard, in full dress, rendered full honors to the President at the camp gates. One of the first things the family did was to walk around the place looking at everything and allowing their two white collies to get some exercise. Oscar Otis, camp caretaker, took them for their first boat ride.

Orman Doty was the guide selected to take the President fishing. Orman was a registered guide and was not a drinking man, so after a full investigation he was the one who spent nearly every day fishing with Coolidge, from July seventh, when he arrived, until he left in the middle of September. Coolidge had not fished since he was a boy, according to Orman, so it was necessary to teach him how to cast. This they did from the dock and pretty soon the President was able to cast out and thumb the reel so as not to get into a backlash.

One day the two were out fishing and the President decided he wanted to smoke. They were near Cranford Island, a real fine pike area, and the President had thrown out his plug and just laid down his pole across his lap. Just as he lit his cigar, a big splash came where his plug was and away went his pole into the lake. That ended his fishing and smoking at the same time. Of course he lost the pole and the fish as well.

Orman said, of this summers' work with Coolidge, that he felt that he had been able to show the President a good bit about the area.

Moses Follensby was one of the earliest settlers in the town. He was supposed to have been a trapper, but no one knew where he had come from and in the end no one knew where he disappeared to. He camped at various locations in the area,, and there are three ponds that bear his name. He first camped and trapped on the shore of Church Pond and also on Lower St. Regis. Then he moved to Follensby, Jr. where he built a permanent camp. He had a dog that was always with him. A man from Keeses Mill area visited him frequenty and Follensby was often seen by the folks from McColloms who passed that way on the road to Brandon to do their shopping or take the train. Brandon was the shopping center at that time. Suddenly in 1823 he was seen no more. The friend told people that Follensby had gone away on a trap, but he never returned and the fact that he had not taken his gun and dog seemed very strange. There was the remains of a meal on the table and two plates which

178

showed he had had company at that meal. For years there was great speculation and many rumors about what became of him. Many believed that he was the victim of foul play and the friend was suspected, as he had the gun. Not much investigation was made, however, and it remains one of the unsolved mysteries.

Mrs. Levi Noble, mother of Hattie Gillespie, told the story of a harrowing experience in her childhood days. She, her parents, and her sister were traveling from Malone to Bloomingdale, or perhaps to Vermontsville, with horses and sleigh. When they reached Mountain Pond the sleigh broke down, so her father had to unhitch the team and ride to Paul Smiths, leaving his family in the sleigh. Of course they were well bundled up and had fur robes, but it grew dark very soon and the baby began to cry. Then in the distance they heard the howl of a wolf and soon it was joined by others coming over the mountain. The wolves kept coming nearer and nearer. Of course the family were frightened to death and her mother could do nothing but pray. Then finally the heard the joyful sound of sleigh-bells and someone coming to get them. In the morning when her father returned to get the sleigh, the wolves had been there and torn the fur robes to pieces. This happened over 125 years ago.

Some Cold Facts About Brighton

1910-1911   John St. Germaine recorded the first snow on November 13, 1910, and by February 2, 1911, 90 inches had fallen at Paul Smiths.

1902-1903   This was a heavy snow winter, 132 inches fell. This was the winter that Paul Smith claimed snow up to his armpits was the usual thing.

1919   The newspaper in February reported that there was too little snow to haul logs from the woods. Not having enough snow to skid them, logs had to be hauled by wagon and this was very costly.

A late winter pastime involved wagering on when the ice would go out of St. Regis Lake. The following tabulations records the official dates accepted locally:

1909—April 16	1922—April 20	1934—April 24
1910—March 31	1923—May 3	1935—April 27
1911—May 2	1924—April 29	1936—April 15
1912—April 26	1925—April 25	1937—April 23
1913—April 19	1926—May 8	1938—April 20
1914—May 1	1927—April 18	1939—May 6
1915—April 20	1928—May 8	1940—May 4
1916—April 28	1929—April 13	1941—April 19
1917—April 30	1930—May 1	1942—April 24
1918—April 30	1931—April 16	1943—May 7
1919—April 16	1932—May 3	1944—May 3
1920—April 27	1933—April 27	1945—March 31
1921—April 5		

Mountain View Cemetery

at

Gabriels, New York — Franklin County

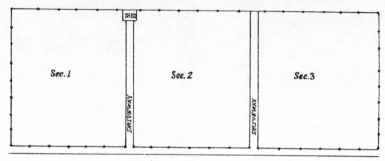

Main Highway

Headstone Information to January, 1970

Sec.

Sec.	Name	Dates
1	Abare, Ada Redwood	1916-1959
1	Alexander, Joseph F.	1878-1955
2	Alexander, Julia A.	1884-1950
1	Alexander, Jessie	1883-1956
1	Alexander, Flora	Jan. 3, 1923
2	Alphonso, Marion Jaquis	1905-1943—wife of Morris
1	Alexander, Ella L.	1880-1931
1	Amell, Philip	1909-1918
1	Amell, Rose	1891-1918
2	Baker, George J.	1936-1938
2	Beaney, Phil H.	1903-1967
2	Beaney, Anna M.	1915-1958
3	Begor, Minnie P.	1900-1968
1	Blanchard, Katie G.	Sept. 23, 1887-Jan. 13, 1889—dau. of Frank and Sarah
3	Buckley, George H., Sr.	Mar. 14, 1893-July 24-1968—N.Y. Sgt., Co. L, 303 Inf. WWI
3	Buckley, George H., Jr.	Jan. 19, 1933-July 4, 1966—N.Y. Cpl., Trans. Corps, USAR
1	Buckley, John J.	1885-1956
1	Bunker, Albert E.	1895-1954
1	Burns, Thomas F.	1874-1920
1	Burns, Bertha Titus	1881-19....
3	Bronfiel, Daniel M.	d 1958
2	Bryant, Percy D.	June 12, 1897-June 5, 1960—N.Y. SFC, 141 Pursuit Sq., Air SVC, WWI
2	Bryant, Carolyn B.	1907-1939
2	Bryant, Jess H.	1882-1943
2	Bryant, Lillian E.	June 21, 1864-Dec. 31-1903—wife of D. F. B.
1	Brink, Sarah A.	1829-1909—wife of Chester

181

Sec.	Name	Dates
1	Brink, Reuben C.	d May 8, 1888—36 years old
1	Brink, Charles E.	d May 9, 1890—20 years old, son of G & S
1	Brink, Chester	d Nov. 6, 1888—63 years old
2	Cochran, Alice Donah	1907-1943
4	Dewey, Eva B.	Nov. 16, 1899-Nov. 18, 1930
3	Doty, Vaughn O.	May 11, 1946-Jan. 13, 1969—N.Y. Sp. 4, 1 Cavalry Div., Vietnam, BSM-PH
1	Downs, Charles W.	1865-1950
1	Downs, Sarah J.	1868-1961
1	Downs, Arthur J.	Dec. 20, 1892-July 2, 1960—N.Y. Pvt., 326 Field Sig. SVC Bn., WWI
2	Duprea, Ollie E.	1885-1959
3	Durrett, Sherman	1910-1959
2	Farrington, Alice Marie	Aug. 5, 1925-Dec. 1, 1926
3	Finlayson, Donald M.	1892-1959
2	Flanders, Robert C.	Dec. 8, 1915-July 17, 1967—N.Y. Cpl., U.S. Army, WWII
1	Flynn, John F.	1916-1945
1	Foshay, Clarence W.	1869-1952
3	Fountain, George W.	1903-1962
1	Fountain, Willard W.	1874-1946
2	Fribance, William George	1876-1950
3	Finlayson, Gertrude M.	1896-1968—wife of Donald
3	Gardner, Roger Dale	1942-1961
1	Gonyea, Philmore	1864-1924
1	Gonyea, Ettie Pritchard	1875-1947
1	Goodell, Elijah	d Jan. 20, 1871—91 years of age
	Goodell, Florence A.	d Oct. 11, 1867—age 5 yrs. Dau. of C. E. and A. (stone broken and stored)
2	Hall, Leman A.	d Sept. 18, 1961—son of J. & M .Hall, 12 yrs. old
3	Helley, Michael	1884-1968
2	Higgins, Arthur J.	1896-1952—WW I
2	Hill, Beatrice M. Otis	1911-1948—wife of Arthur
1	Hobart, Benjamine F.	1832-1892
1	Hobart, Louisa H. Newell	1835-1894
1	Hobart, Henry N.	1863-1931
1	Hobart, Frank B.	1892-1966
1	Hobart, Stella Downs	1895-1947
1	Hobart, Kathryn Daly	1897-1965
3	Hogan, William J.	1897-1967
3	Howley, Reginald	June 11, 1911-Nov. 15, 1969—N.Y. S2, USNR, WW II
2	Hyde, H. M.	1862-1910
2	Hyde, Ada Shene	1869-1950—wife of H. M.
	Hobart, James M.	d Jan. 20, 1863—age 27 yrs. (stone broken and stored)
2	Jacobs, Perley E.	July 22, 1899-Mar. 14, 1967
2	Jacobs, Teresa	July 9, 1897-Oct. 26, 1967
2	Jacquis, Ernest I.	1901-1959
2	Jacquis, Charles W.	1872-1926
1	Jenkins, Charles H.	1857-1938
1	Jenkins, Annie Delameter	1864-1922
1	Jenkins, C. J.	1834-1907
1	Jenkins, Sarah	July 15, 1833-Feb. 25, 1872—wife of C.J.
1	Jenkins, Nettie	1864-1943
1	Jenkins, Rose	1870-1949

1	Jenkins, George E.	Aug. 31, 1862-May 20, 1892—son of C.J.
1	Jenkins, Willie	Dec. 13, 1865-Jan. 11, 1866—son of C.J. & S.
1	Jenkins, Sewell	Feb. 10, 1867-Feb. 12, 1867—son of C.J. & S.
1	Jenkins, Sarah	Feb. 18, 1872-July 19, 1872—dau. of C.J. & S.
1	Jenkins, Charles	d Nov. 25, 1899—2 months old, son of J.E. & E.
1	Jester, Penny Lee	1955-1955
1	Jones, Arthur T.	1894-1956
1	Jones, Clark Rork	1911-1959
1	Jenkins, George B.	Nov. 25, 1899—age 11 yrs., son of J.E. & E.
2	Kerry, Phelps Smith	d Dec. 22, 1896—(stone broken, age lost)
2	King, Ambrose	d Feb. 10, 1866—age 69
2	King, Mary Magdalene	d Apr. 11, 1876—(stone broken, no age visible)
2	King, Philmon J.	d Aug. 28, 1880—age 6 mo., son of Philmon & June
2	King, John	d July 13, 1863—son of Philmon & June (no age)
2	King, Philemon	1838-1908
2	King, Jane J. Quarters	1841-1911—wife of Philemon
2	King, Ralph W.	d Oct. 22, 1900—age 1 yr., son of J.O. & B.M.
1	King, Emery B.	1910-1920
1	Labounty, Charley A.	d Feb. 2, 1872—son of Geo. & L.
2	Lafountain, Bert	1886-1959
2	Lafountain, Charlotte	1889-1949—wife of Bert
2	Lafountain, Mabelle	1913-1928
1	Leavitt, Charles I.	Nov. 23, 1888-Apr. 17, 1968—N.Y. Pvt. Field Hosp. 20, WW I
1	Leavitt, Lyman A.	1843-1926
1	Leavitt, Ada E. Jenkins	1858-1924—wife of L.A.
1	Leavitt, Arthur	1884-1969
1	Leavitt, Eleanor McMaster	1881-1958—wife of A.
2	Long, Vernon E.	Mar. 11, 1867-Mar. 1, 1943
2	Long, Sarah A. Taylor	Feb. 11, 1833-Jan. 21, 1908
2	Lund, Sylvia Jaquis	1879-1955
2	Lyon, Rufus	d Nov. 27, 1891—age 48
2	Lyons, Lois	1853-1948
2	Lyons, Richard R.	d Dec. 1, 1887—68 yrs. old
2	Lyon, Adelia Spear	d May 13, 1882—Age 62 yrs., wife of Richard R.
2	Lyon, Carrie	d May 15, 1878—(infant) daughters of
2	Lyon, Mary	d Dec. 3, 1876—(infant) G. & A. Lyon
1	MacDonald, Archibald	Sept. 9, 1886-Jan. 31, 1951—N.Y. Pvt. 319 Inf., 80 Div. Co. G, WW I
1	Macy, Frank A.	1863-1933
1	Macy, Rose Amell	1879-1958
1	Macy, Frank A.	1894-1967—son of F.A. & R.
2	McDermid, Walter S.	1869-1929
2	McDermid, Kate B. King	1871-1919
1	McLaughlin, John F.	1840-1911
1	McLaughlin, Mary S. Otis	1838-1937—wife of J.F.
2	Martin, Hugh	d Set. 27, 1881—age 72 yrs.

2	Martin, Sally Goodell	d Sept. 26, 1880—age 69 yrs., wife of Hugh
2	Martin, Henry H.	1887-1918
2	Martin, Edgar	1899-1919
2	Martin, Addie	1860-1933
1	Martin, Douglas E.	1846-1926
1	Martin, Nora J. Rork	1855-1901—wife of D.E.
3	Martin, Douglass E.	1895-1958
3	Martin, Abbie E.	1891-1965
3	Martin, Adelaide I.	1905-1964
2	Martin, Margaret McDonald	1904-1957—wife of Benjamin
2	Martin, Fred E., Jr.	1885-1898
2	Martin, Fred E., Sr.	1850-1923
1	Martin, Allen William	d Dec. 8, 1947—son of Lea & Agnes
1	Martin, John H.	1872-1951
3	Minty, Russell J.	Sept. 19, 1900-Jan. 3, 1965—Iowa Brig. Gen., US Air Force, WWII, DSM
1	Martin, Daniel Earl	Jan. 21, 1956-Jan. 24-1956—son B & H
2	Morey, Millie	1884-1966
1	Morris, Lucius R., Jr.	Jan. 10, 1899-July 14, 1910—son of L. & D.
1	Mulligan, Harry B.	1870-1935
2	Muncil, Lottie H.	1892-1967
2	Muncil, Joyce A.	1935-1936
1	Newell, Joseph W.	1838-1883
1	Newell, Paulina B. Hobart	1846-1922—wife of Joseph W.
1	Newell, Clarisa H.	d May 26, 1880—age 75 yrs., wife of John
1	Newell, Blake S.	1902-1968
1	Newell, Joseph L.	June 15, 1823-Mar. 8, 1905
1	Newell, Maria G.	1859-1916
1	Newell, Eva L.	Sept. 20, 1860-May 21, 1948
1	Newell, Sylvester A.	Oct. 31, 1855-May 26, 1918
1	Newell, Eliza H.	July 11, 1885 (?)—wife of Lovel P., age 25 yrs. (?)
2	Nobel, H. J.	d July 22, 1878—age 78
2	O'Donall, Hugh	d June 7, 1883—age 31
2	O'Donall, Lidia	d May 15, 1882—age 26, wife of Hugh
3	Oliver, Diane	1960-1960
2	O'Neil, Mirium Demis	d Sept. 28, 1855—age 5 mo., dau. of Thomas & Lucy
2	Ormsby, Rudolph W.	1897-1916
1	Ormsby, Hannah	d Apr. 23, 1921—age 76, wife of Stephen
1	Ormsby, William	d Mar. 3, 1895—age 23, son of Stephen & Hannah
3	Oshier, Edward M.	1910-1968
3	Otis, William A.	1898-1959
3	Otis, Rebecca Joe	1961 (infant)
2	Otis, Frank W.	1901-1958
2	Otis, Gordon	1903-1966
2	Otis, Henry A.	1868-1934
2	Otis, Bertha Covel	1874-1960
2	Otis, Harriett O.	d Nov. 14, 1870—wife of William
	Otis, Hazel A.	d Sept. 20, 1895—age 11 mos., dau. Albert & Mary (stone broken, stored)
	Otis, _____	d Dec. 7, 1883—infant son of Orin & Samantha (stone stored, broken)
2	Otis, Charles F.	d Jan. 15, 1866—age 7, son of William & Harriett

Sec.		
2	Otis, William O.	d Sept. 23, 1902—age 77
2	Otis, Celestia L.	Wife of Wm. O.
2	Otis, Eliza P.	d Aug. 18, 1887—infant
2	Otis, William Henry	Apr. 11, 1876
1	Otis, Alfred	1905-1966
1	Otis, Mildred Clary	1905-1954—wife of Alfred
1	Otis, Joshua	d Jan. 10, 1882—78 yrs.
1	Otis, Amy Manning	d Sept. 20, ...—age 71,wife of Joshua
1	Otis, Henry M.	d July 16, 1864—age 22
1	Otis, Silas F.	d July 5, 1863—age 3
1	Otis, Lillian B.	d July 25, 1873—age 3 mo.
1	Otis, Ellian B.	d May 19, 1873—3 weeks old
1	Otis, Alfred H.	1850-1931
1	Otis, Ruth N. Chase	1854-1924
1	Otis, Joshua A.	d July 18, 1894—age 24, son of A.H. & R.N.
1	Otis, Almond F.	d Jan. 14, 1869—age 5 mo., son of Myron & Mina
2	Owen, Deziah Miller	d Mar. 22, 1901—age 89, wife of Harry
1	Otis, Samantha A. Newell	1847-1905—wife of Oren
1	Otis, Oren	1849-1914
1	Otis (infant)	1901—son of O. & S.
2	Palmer, Lon	d Sept. 2, 1896—age 39 yrs.
2	Paquin, Dawn Helen	1953-1954
2	Paquin, Howard R.	June 19, 1950-Apr. 18, 1969—N.Y. L Cpl H & S Co. 26 Mar 9 MAB Vietnam PH
1	Park, Charles Edwin	Mar. 26, 1908-Nov. 22, 1969—NY Pvt. Hq. BN 1 Calv.
2	Patterson, J. N.	1857-
2	Patterson, Margaret	1846-1918
2	Patterson, Perley	d Jan. 30, 1882—age 6 mos.—son of J. N. & M.
2	Patterson, Scott	1875-1965
2	Patterson, Armene I.	1888-1957
1	Pearson, Frank P.	1884-
1	Pearson, Alida D.	1876-1955
1	Paye, Bernard L.	June 9, 1888-Mar. 21, 1951—N.Y. Pvt. Army Srevice Corp. WW I
1	Paye, Doris E.	1920-1921—dau. of William & Mina
1	Paye, William L.	1875-1942
1	Paye, S. L.	1846-1929
1	Paye, Mary L.	1848-1919
1	Paye, F. S.	1883-1912
2	Perrino, Diane May	Sept. 23, 1949-Oct. 20, 1949
2	Perry, Leona	1892-1934—wife of Frederick
2	Perry, Emily	1893-1966
1	Prellwitz, William R.	Apr. 2, 1867-May 14, 1899 —Veteran
1	Pudvah, Ben	
2	Quain, Arthur	1880-1938
2	Quarter, Sophia	d Feb. 21, 1858—age 21, dau. of Julious & Betsey
2	Quarter, John	d Oct. 20, 1862—age 24, son of Julious & Betsey
2	Quarter, Justus	d Feb. 15, 1863—age 20, son of Julious & Betsey
1	Quarter, William H.	d Feb. 13, 1892—age 22 yrs.
1	Quarter, Charles H.	d Mar. 8, 1901—age 54 yrs.

185

	Quarter, Mary A.	d Feb. 14, 1870—age 7 days, dau. of C. H. & S. L. (stone broken & stored)
2	Premo, Jennie	1834-1954
2	Premo, Albert	1883-1937
2	Premo, Leo E.	1905-1952
2	Premo, Ella H.	1890-1927
1	Redwood, Ann	d June 20, 1886—age 52 yrs.
1	Redwood, John	d Mar. 17, 1880—age 72 yrs.
1	Redwood, Bridget	d Nov. 19, 1861
1	Redwood, William J.	d Jan. 2, 1862—age 9 yrs.
3	Redwood, Leon	Nov. 21, 1927-Sept. 1, 1968—N.Y. 188 Prcht. Inf. II ABN Div., WWII
1	Redwood, Lucena E. Estes	1854-1911—wife of Thomas
1	Redwood, John L.	1882-1962
2	Reyell, Clifford F.	1902-1966
1	Reyome, Charles	1880-1954
1	Ricketson, Mary	d Aug. 26, 1846—age 43, wife of George
1	Ricketson, Roba E.	d Aug. 21, 1869—age 51, wife of George
1	Ricketson, William	d Oct. 29, 1891—age 86 yrs.
1	Ricketson, Abigal B.	d May 31, 1904—age 84, wife of William
1	Ricketson, Richard B.	d Jan. 22, 1897—age 62 yrs.
1	Ricketson, Margaret A.	d Feb. 1, 1913—age 57 yrs.
1	Ricketson, Elbridge G.	d Nov. 1, 1916—age 67 yrs.
1	Ricketson, Alice Hall	d Oct. 6, 1926—age 75, wife of Elbridge
1	Ricketson, Caleb S.	d Mar. 16, 1872—age 26, son of Wm. & Abigal
1	Ricketson, Charles C.	d Oct. 19, 1863—age 11, son of Wm. & Abigal
1	Ricketson, Alice I.	d Dec. 11, 1861—age 1 yr., dau. of Wm. & Abigal
1	Ricketson, Nelson W.	d Jan. 8, 1862—age 23, son of Wm. & Hannah
1	Ricketson, Edna	d Dec. 17, 1860—infant dau. of Nelson & Rachel
1	Riley, George B.	1882-1951
1	Riley, Charles J.	1875-1950
1	Riley, Mary E.	1875-1958—wife of Charles J.
1	Robare, Harold	d Nov. 14, 1940—N.Y. Pvt 153 Depot Brig
1	Robare, Frank	d Apr. 6, 1895—age 37 yrs.
2	Robare, Halsey F.	1879-1944
2	Robare, Richard	1882-1919
2	Robare, Ernest M.	1885-1935
2	Robare, Margaret	1883-1947
2	Robare, Sophia Ella	d Apr. 17, 1874—dau. of Z. & M.
2	Robare, Beatrice Davis	1886-1958
3	Rogers, Ward M.	1884-1953
2	Rochester, John E.	1889-1950
2	Rochester, Jennie E.	1886-1952
2	Rochester, Jane	1919-1926
2	Rochester, Marion	1918-1928
1	Rork, Clara A.	July 18, 1893-Oct. 18, 1904
1	Rork, George H.	Mar. 30, 1862-Oct. 15, 1906
1	Rork, Clara A. Hobart	Feb. 15, 1865-Aug. 14, 1895—wife of George H.
1	Rork, Laura	May 27, 1895-June 30, 1895
1	Rork, Henry	1888-1939
1	Rork, Sarah C. Sprague	1888-1932—wife of Henry

Sec.		
1	Rork, George A., Sr.	1916-1962
1	Rork, Clarence A.	1889-1951
1	Rork, Margaret A. Coyle	1884-1946—wife of Clarence A.
1	Rork, Frederick W.	1865-1918
1	Rork, Edward	d July 29, 1898—age 75 yrs.
1	Rork, Clara	d Mar. 26, 1881—age 50, wife of Edward
2	Russell, Jennie Robare	1861-1912—wife of M. Russell
1	St. Germain, Lafayette	d Dec. 9, 1877—age 26
1	Sawyer, Kate Hewitt	1846-1882—wife of Moses E.
2	Schrader, August E.	1893-1954
2	Schrader, Hulda E.	1893-1949
1	Selkirk, Nettie	1872-1953
1	Simpson, Florence	1910-1950
3	Shanty, Herbert	Aug. 7, 1892-Apr. 12, 1967—Pfc. 346 GD & Fire Co. QMC WW I
1	Skiff, James A.	1868-1935
1	Skiff, Fannie E. Tyler	d Mar. 29, 1895—age 19 yrs.
2	Smith, Willard S.	1863-1942
2	Smith, Delia Prespare	1876-1944—wife of Willard S.
1	Smith, Sarah	1880-1966
1	Sparkes, William H.	1881-1968
2	Sprague, Warren	1854-1924
2	Sprague, Adwena Swinyer	1854-1934
1	Strack, Louis P.	1860-1938
1	Strack, Emma Grenier	1873-1926—wife of Louis P.
1	Stern, Margaret	1885-1961
1	Stern, Joseph	1878-1955
1	Stern, David B.	Aug. 3, 1912-Aug. 3, 1957—NY Pvt. US Army WW II
1	Stern, Iris	1917-1967
3	Symonds, Lloyd J.	June 25, 1918-Apr. 15, 1965—NY Pfc. US Army WW II BSM
1	Skiff, (twins)	1952
3	Symonds, Clarence E.	June 25, 1919-Oct. 2, 1968
2	Tebo, Charles F.	July 29, 1894-July 5, 1966—NY Sgt. US Army WW I
2	Tebo, Ambrose A., Jr.	1876-1963
2	Tebo, Louis H.	1879-1944
2	Tebo, Lillian A.	1893-1924—wife of Louis
2	Tebo, Charles	1920-1944—son of Louis & Lillian
2	Tebo, Ambrose A.	July 28, 1849-Mar. 7, 1925
2	Tebo, Philomen Blaze	July 29, 1844-Aug. 8, 1929
2	Toof, Fred C.	1881-1915
2	Toof, Louise Thelma	d June 9, 1909—age 3 yrs. dau. of Fred
2	Toof, Lula W.	1873-1914
3	Tucker, Joseph J.	June 2, 1886-Mar. 2, 1963—Pvt. Co. A, 2 Anti Acft MG BN WW I
1	Titus, Lula A.	June 15, 1907-Nov. 12, 1907
1	Titus, M. Katherine	d Oct. 5, 1900—infant dau. J. H. & B.A.
3	Tyler, Deborah Ann	Mar. 4, 1951-Oct. 27, 1960
2	Tyler, Abner	d Nov. 13, 1904—age 61 yrs. 6 mos. Co. C118 Reg. NY
2	Tyler, Lemira Muncil	1853-1932—wife of Abner
1	Tyler, Herbert E.	1889-1955
1	Tyler, Clara E. Martin	1884-1944—wife of Herbert E.
1	Tyler, John H., Jr.	1875-1909
1	Underhill, Irving E.	1885-1935

3	Villnave, Emma	1873-1959
2	Walsh. Joseph F.	1881-1963
2	Walsh, Effie Melvin	1881-1930—wife of Joseph F.
2	Walton, Frederick C.	1881-1947
1	Wardner. Frank M.	1863-1925
1	Wardner, Lydia M.	1865-1956
1	Wardner, Axie Clouie	d Feb. 9, 1889—age 7 mos., dau. of A.M. & P.A.
1	Wardner, William H.	d Dec. 6, 1888—age 68 yrs.
1	Wardner, Clara A. Duntley	Oct. 16, 1827-Sept. 20, 1911—wife of Wm. H.
1	Wardner, Seth	d Sept. 25, 1898—age 75 yrs.
1	Wardner, James M.	Aug. 15, 1831-Nov. 15, 1904
1	Wardner, Addie S.	Jan. 1, 1851-June 1, 1907—wife of James M.
1	Wardner, Delia M.	d June 7, 1871—age 35 yrs.
1	Wardner, Phoebe M.	d Aug. 8, 1876—age 82 yrs., wife of Nathan
1	Watson, Mamie E.	1880-1938
1	Watson. Alberte	Feb. 13, 1904-Oct. 22, 1904—son of J & N
1	Watson, Martin M.	1843-1902
2	Weller, Samuel	d Aug. 15, 1858—age 62 yrs.
2	Weller. Annis	d May 24, 1879—age 82, wife of Samuel
2	Weller, Freelon B.	d Feb. 6, 1892—age 56 yrs.
2	Weller. Sarah Owen	d April 18, 1911—age 70 yrs.
2	Weller, Thomas O.	d Feb. 15, 1897—age 35 yrs.
2	Williams, William J.	1872-1939
1	Woods. Thomas H.	1885-1956
2	Wheeler, Charles H.	1870-1938
1	Yell. Edmond	1877-1949
1	Yell, Cora	1885-196 —wife of Edmond

McCollom's Cemetery

Town of Brighton — at

McColloms, New York — Franklin County

Headstone Information

Delametter, Julius	1828-1913
Delametter, Elbridge	1864-1916
Delametter, Edith	1896-1911
Delametter, Katharine	1905-1931
Delametter, Amanda	1826-1912
Ferguson. Floyd F.	Feb. 2, 1893-Apr. 26-1964—Pvt. NY Co. B, 348 Inf., WW I
Hinkson, Maurace	1905-1925
Hinkson. David	1869-1919
Jost, Joseph J.	Nov. 2, 1965-Nov. 3, 1965
McArthur, Clarence A.	1852-1913
McArthur, Cecile V. Hutchins	1858-1941—wife of C.A.

Sec.

McArthur, Nora Pearl	1885- —dau. of C.A. & C.V.
McArthur, Harry W.	1883-1885—son of C.A. & C.V.
McArthur, Earl C.	July 15, 1888-May 24, 1965
McArthur, Gladys R.	Aug. 11, 1886-May 12, 1965
McCollom, Amiel C.	Jan. 21, 1819-Aug. 23, 1893—father
McCollom, Eliza Ann	Oct. 12, 1816-Mar. 29, 1892—wife
McCollom, Amiel C.	d Oct. 1, 1861—age 10 yrs. — son
McCollom, Joseph Chandler	d Jan. 2, 1862—age 14 yrs. 10 mos. — son
McCollom, Charles C.	d Sept. 2, 1861—age 17 yrs. — son
McCollom, Freelove Orphena	d Sept. 12, 1861 — age 8 yrs. — dau.
McCollom, Eliza Ann	d Apr. 28, 1852 — age 7 mos. — dau.
Miner, John B.	d Sept. 7, 1882 — age 31 yrs.
Roser, Judith Ann	1969 — infant
Summers, C. Henry	1867-1934
Summers, Emorett Putnam	1872-1941—wife of C.H.
Tyler, Viola	d Nov. 5, 1873—age 5 yrs., dau. of A & L

St. John's in the Wilderness Cemetery

at

Paul Smiths, New York — Franklin County

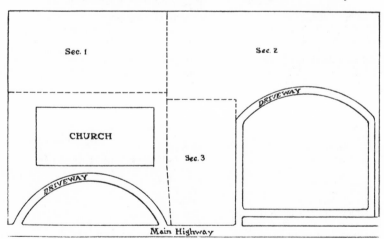

Headstone Information to January, 1970

Sec.

2	Abare, Louis H.	1888-1948
2	Anderson, Donald	Aug. 12, 1912-Nov. 24, 1963—NY Tec 5, 901 Signal Co., WW II
1	Armstrong, Marguerite de Longue	1867-1932—wife of C. R. Armstrong
3	Beaney, Roger Paul	1927-1930
3	Beaney, Phil Francis	1924-1930
3	Beaney, Frances L.	1904-1951

189

2	Betters, James J.	1853-1936
2	Betters, Marian Marshall	1860-1948
3	Betters, Levi J.	1880-1967
3	Betters, Vina LeBeau	1884-1962—wife of Levi
3	Betters, Madeline A.	1906-1938—dau. of Levi & Vina
2	Betters, Clifford H.	1903-1957
3	Benentt, Lucy A. Stave	d Dec. 22, 1889—age 47 yrs.
3	Bennett, Phineaus H.	d 1892—(no age given)
3	Bennett, Alva A.	July 4, 1870-Mar. 17, 1931
3	Bennett, Donald A.	Jan. 12, 1912-Feb. 25, 1914
2	Bickford, Sandra Jane	1947-1960
2	Bigelow, Gladys M.	1897-1967
3	Bigelow, Eliza Presper	Feb. 19, 1863-Feb. 19, 1917
3	Block, Sadie	1897-1933
2	Bomyea, Charles O.	1893-1966
2	Blanchard, John	Jan. 5, 1895-Jan. 23, 1967—NY Pvt. US Army WW I
1	Blanchard, Earl F.	Nov. 3, 1898-Oct. 26, 1917
1	Blanchard, Ned	May 25, 1902-July 7, 1906—son of F. & S.
1	Blanchard, Anna	June 21, 1905-July 6, 1905—dau. of F. & S.
1	Blanchard, Frank X.	1857-1941
1	Blanchard, Sarah Sawyer	1861-1943—wife of Frank X.
1	Brown, Jeannette M. Cox	1892-1952—wife of James C.
1	Buck, Edmund M.	1873-1951
1	Buck Halcyon H.	1870-1952—wife of E.M.
1	Buck, Halcyon Louise	1909-1929—dau. of E. M. & H.
1	Buchanan, Joseph	Mar. 31, 1865-Oct. 11, 1944—(born in Adrian, Mich.)
1	Butler, John H.	1905-1945
1	Byrd, Samuel Wyman	Aug. 24, 1872-Sept. 17, 1892
1	Byrd, Mary Wyman	Apr. 20, 1863-July 3, 1893
3	Choules, Arthur B.	1866-1932
3	Choules, Mary A.	1872-1968
3	Claremont, Marie	no dates for infant
3	Clark, Polly	d Sept. 1, 1898—age 41 yrs., wife of T. N. Clark
1	Connors, John	1866-1923
1	Connors, Leo	d Apr. 8, 1912—infants of Bertha M.
1	Connors, Leon	d Apr. 8, 1912 McLane Connors
3	Cooper, Joseph Marin	1873-1956
3	Cooper, Margaret Van Nest	1877-1956
1	Crary, Orvis R.	1860-1938
1	Crary, Martha M. Swinyer	1862-1928
3	Cross, William H.	1874-1922
3	Cross, Catherine Garry	1876-1948—wife of Wm. H.
3	Cross, James M.	1844-1908
3	Cross, Albertine H.	1864-1918
3	Curtin, William J.	1896-1924
3	David, Peter	1860-1906
3	Davis, Donna C.	1848-1955
3	Disotell, Cecilia Paquin	Feb. 22, 1899-June 10, 1958
1	Distin, Ethel Brown	1883-1959
1	Donaldson, Loretta M.	1911-1953
1	Donaldson, Charles	1869-1942
2	Donaldson, Harold C.	1900-1960

Sec.		
1	Doyle, Nina Mae Durham	Nov. 1898-July 1936
1	Drake, Josie M.	1888-1943
2	Drew, Walter E.	1894-1949
1	Eckart, Harry S.	1871-1951
1	Eckart, Louise M.	1875-1962
1	Eckart, Harold C.	July 9, 1898-Jan. 2, 1957—Ill. 2nd Lt. Fa. Res. WW I
1	Farrar, Carl B.	1886-1955
1	Farrar, Maud G.	1887-1967
1	Farrar, Laura E.	1923-1925—dau. of Carl & Maud
2	Farrar, Frank L.	1921-1962
2	Farrar, Beverly K.	1948-1965—dau. of Frank & Katherine
1	Field, Stephany	Dec. 15, 1890-Aug. 12, 1901
2	Finlayson, Arnold R.	Aug. 21, 1917-May 5, 1960—NY Tech 4 11 Replacement Depot WW II
1	Fisher, Mary Hunsicker	1874-1933
1	Fisher, George Kingsbury	1865-1940
1	Fisher, Emily	1867-1955
1	Fitzpatric, John Henry	1891-Oct. 5, 1937—NY Corp. 52 Pioneer Inf.
3	Flockhart, James	1853-1939
3	Flockhart, Margaret Drysdale	1854-1937
3	Flockhart, Richard H.	1906-1942
2	Gallagher, Robert	Apr. 15, 1913-May 3, 1965—N.Y. Tech 4 Ordinance Dpt. WW II
1	Galt, Eleanor Hall	1901-1934
1	Galt, (Mother)	1869-1945
3	Gallagher, Mary Martha	1857-1926
3	Gallagher, Robert	1885-1929
3	Gallagher, Ola E.	1889-1959
2	Gardiner, Richard W.	1874-1953
2	Gardiner, Mona A.	1908-1955—dau. of Richard W.
2	Gardner, Leroy Upson	1888-1946
1	Garvey, Jess E. F.	1885-1910
1	Garvey, Katie E. Crary	1884-1959—wife of Jess
3	Gleisner, Charles J.	1883-1956
3	Gleisner, Daisey A.	1878-1959—wife of Charles J.
2	Goddard, Thomas J.	1882-1959
3	Hartz, Margaret Parker	1907-1936
1	Hickok, Leah Martin	May 27, 1886-May 27, 1912—wife of Halsey
1	Hall, George H.	Oct. 9, 1869-June 15, 1948
1	Hall, Elizabeth Marshall	Oct. 19, 1871-Mar. 1, 1946
2	Hall, Elias E.	1845-1914
2	Hall, Phoeba A.	1848-1921—wife of Elias E.
2	Hall, John	June 7, 1893—age 73 yrs.
2	Harding, John	1862-1938
2	Harding, Emma Thomas	1862-1953
1	Harris, Charles Cuthbert	Dec. 23, 1886-Mar. 31, 1959
1	Heise, Frederick H. (Dr.)	1883-1946—(from Baltimore, Md. and at Trudeau San.)
3	Henderson, Janet Louise	Sept. 30, 1877-Oct. 12, 1958—dau. of Charles R. & Jeane H.
2	Holcombe, Charlene	1888-1964
2	Hourihan, Jerry	1898-1967
3	Jaquis, Irving	1844-1915
3	Jaquis, Jane M.	1884-1887—wife of Irving

191

Sec.	Name	Dates
3	Jaquis, Loana B.	Feb. 19, 1869-Dec. 12, 1929
3	Jaquis, John B.	d May 11, 1917—age 45 yrs.
3	Jaquis, Carrie	(no date)—age 17 mos., dau. of John & Carrie
3	Jaquis, Richard C.	1933-1938
3	Jerman, Llewellyn D.	1876-1938
2	Kay, Jeane Werner	1922-1967
3	Kirche, Charles	1884-1966
3	Kirche, Janet C. Moyer	1889-1937—wife of Charles
3	Kirche, John & Frederick	1944- —sons of C. D. & C.
1	Kirk, Muriel	1902-1930
2	Law, James W.	1919-1968
3	LaBombard, Clifford G.	Feb. 14, 1950-Apr. 15, 1969—Marine Pfc. Vietnam
3	Lancaster, Joseph A.	1890-1949
3	Lancaster, Kathryn O.	1888-1963—wife of Joseph
1	LaMay, Theresa	1891-1938
1	LaMay, Wilbert	1884-1924
1	LaMay, Philmen	1854-1932—wife of George
1	LaMay, George	1852-1921
2	Lester, William G.	1957-1963—son of Clarence & Dorothy
2	Little, Walter E.	Nov. 23, 1894-July 22, 1962—Conn. OM3 USNRF WW I
3	Longtemps, Lemira	d June 14, 1901—age 1 yr., dau. of J.D. & L. V.
2	Lusk, Rev. William Brown	1871-1953
2	Lusk, Edna Bright	1884-1963
2	Lusk, William B., Jr.	1919-1949—WW II
2	Lyon, Seth	1867-1943
2	Lyon, Meribah Hutchins	1861-1942
2	Lyon, Herbert F.	July 16, 1893-July 19, 1965—NY Pfc. US Army WW I
2	Mace, Henry F.	1903-1968
3	McCaffrey, William	1859-1912
3	McCaffrey, Mary	Nov. 19, 1861-July 21, 1950—wife of William
1	Mahler, Eugenia White	1886-1946
2	MacIntyre, George H.	1908-1962
1	McLane, Estella W.	1855-1898
2	MacIntyre, James	Sept. 26, 1879-Dec. 11, 1970—Navy Lt. WW I and WW II
2	MacIntyre, Mary Elizabeth	Mar. 14, 1874-Feb. 12, 1966
3	Malstrom, Isabel Smith	1909-1958
3	Marshall, Joseph	d May 13, 1898—age 73 yrs.
3	Marshall, Harriet	d Feb. 19, 1922—age 86 yrs.
1	Martin, Earl W.	Dec. 1, 1917-Jan. 29, 1960—Tec 5 87 Calvary Recon Sq WW II
1	Martin, Paul S.	1891-1957
1	Martin, Lillian H.	1920-1920—dau. of Paul S. & Lea W.
3	Martin, Hugh	1868-1942
3	Martin, Harriet Derby	1870-1938—wife of Hugh
1	Martin, Henry M.	Jan. 18, 1840-Oct. 30, 1915
1	Martin, Sarah E.	Mar. 19, 1842-June 24, 1914—wife of Henry M.
1	Martin, Cleora E.	Apr. 17, 1875-Nov. 1, 1882
1	Martin, "Baby"	(no dates)
3	Meagher, Cornelius	1891-1950

3	Otis, Oscar James	Jan. 20, 1898-Feb. 25, 1963—NY Pfc. 707 Co. MTC WW I
3	Otis, Louise E. Macinally	1893-1959
3	Otis, Arthur L.	1879-1932
3	Otis, Ruby Sibley	1881-1933—wife of Arthur L.
3	Otis, John	d Oct. 1, 1892—age 56 yrs.
3	Otis, Lucretia	1834-1903
2	Otis, John F.	1897-1924—son of Frank & Jennie
2	Otis, Elmer T.	1887-1938
2	Otis, Frank A.	1865-1901
2	Otis, Jennie M.	1868-1948—wife of Frank A.
3	Otis, Sylvester	d Jan. 17, 1929—age 84 yrs., Co. C, 118th Reg. NY Vol.
3	Otis, Joshua	1828-1929
3	Otis, Albert S.	1855-1928
3	Otis, Mary Colby	1862-1937
3	Otis, Howard	Sept. 4, 1894-Apr. 18, 1955—NY Pvt. Co H, 2 Engr Tng Rgt WW I
1	Otis, Myron J.	May 10, 1848-May 1, 1930
1	Otis, Mina J. Chase	May 24, 1856-Dec. 23, 1925—wife of Myron J.
1	Otis, Harry G.	1874-1946
1	Otis, Jeanette	1874-1948—wife of Harry G.
1	Otis, Katheryn P.	Apr. 30, 1920-Apr. 16, 1922—dau. of Harry & Jeanette
1	Otis, Virginia	Mar. 17, 1901-Apr. 24, 1901—dau. of Harry & Jeanette
2	Palmer, Dean	1887-1942
2	Palmer, Charles Middlebrook	1856-1949
2	Palmer, Mary Sill	1859-1941
1	Palmer, Charles Sill	1885-1946
3	Palmer, Alva J.	d Dec. 17, 1907—age 13 yrs., son of D.B. & C.M.
3	Palmer, Roland D.	d Apr. 13, 1910—age 2 mos., son of D.B. & C.M.
3	Parker, Margaret	1907-1936—wife of John Jacob Hartz
2	Parsons, Hollis S.	May 13, 1906-Aug. 10, 1965—NY S-Sgt. 2538 Base Unit AAF WWII
3	Paye, Martha J.	Apr. 13, 1860-June 16, 1909—wife of Geo. W.
3	Paye, Durward W.	1889-1910
2	Peroni, Paul	1954-1959—son of George & Francis
2	Petterson, Edward W. (Dr.)	July 29, 1873-Oct. 2, 1960
2	Petttis, Clifford Robert	Aug. 10, 1877-Jan. 29, 1927
2	Petttis, Maude Otis	Apr. 10, 1879-Apr. 18, 1954—wife of C.R.
2	Pickett, Howell Grady	Sept. 20, 1899-Feb. 26, 1967—NC Pvt US Army WW I
3	Plank, Rudolph	d Apr. 20, 1941—NY Pvt 3 Serv Co. Sig. Corp
2	Potter, Lyman W.	1892-1952
1	Poyer, William Jaeger	Oct. 17, 1923-Jan. 23 1924
3	Prentice, Henry	1837-1904
3	Prentice, Gracie	d Nov. 13, 1896—age 6 mos., dau. of Henry & Emma
3	Prentice, Lena M.	d Feb. 27, 1898—age 4 mos., dau. of Henry & Emma

3	Parker, Henry Stanley	1878-1954
3	Parker, Margaret Jenkins	1880-1862—wife of Henry S.
1	Quain, Jerome	1868-1941
1	Quain, Cora	1881-1947
3	Quarters, Sophia E.	1855-1921
3	Quarters, Justus M.	1878-1953
3	Quarters, Jennie M.	1866-1950—wife of J.M.
1	Rand, Frederick	1906-1930
1	Ransom, Spafard, Jr.	Sept. 4, 1908-Feb. 16, 1930
1	Ransom, Spafard Hooker (Dr.)	Dec. 13, 1873-Apr. 11, 1957
3	Redwood, Thomas R.	1903-1963
3	Redwood, John P.	June 5, 1896-Sept. 23, 1958
3	Redwood, Sue K.	Nov. 29, 1894-May 12, 1962
3	Redwood, John E.	1863-1941
3	Redwood, M. Irene Hayes	1872-1953
3	Redwood, Marjorie Alta	d Nov. 29, 1901—age 2 mos.—dau. of M. Irene
3	Redwood, Katherine Hayes	d July 29, 1899—age 1 yr.—dau. of Irene
2	Ridenour, John Schell	1882-1965
1	Riggs, Benjamin C. (Dr.)	Feb. 16, 1845-Apr. 18, 1883—(born in St. Louis, Mo.)
1	Riggs, Rebecca Fox	Mar. 16, 1852-July 22, 1937—(born in N. Y. City)
1	Rollins, Carrie E. Jaquis	1877-1946
3	Sawyer, Joseph E.	1883-195
1	Samson, Homer (D.Sc.)	1880-1945
3	Sawyer, Roy R.	1905-1958
3	Sawyer, Edith O.	1911-1967
3	Sawyer, Joseph	1856-19....
3	Sawyer, Agnes L. Emery	1866-1920—wife of Joseph
3	Sawyer, John J.	1883-1946
3	Sawyer, Mabel A. Otis	1883-1953
2	Sawyer, Moses E.	1848-1941
2	Sawyer, Cora S.	1866-1945
3	Sawyer, Emma	1889-1949—wife of Joseph E.
3	Sawyer, Arnold V.	1918-1960
3	Sawyer, J. Ned	1895-1939
3	Schneider, George A.	1878-1958
3	Schneider, Caroline F.	1874-1958
3	Schramm, Henry C.	1880-1940
1	Scofield, Mary G.	1858-1917—(on Sprague lot)
2	Shackett, B. Elaine	July 11, 1916-Oct. 15, 1958
3	Simpson, Charles W.	1875-1967
3	Simpson, Rose Collins	1879-1941—wife of C.W.
1	Slavin, James	1840-1917—Pvt. 16 N.Y. Vols.
1	Slavin, Margaret Delancy	1872-1963
1	Slavin, Edward G.	1877-1920
1	Slavin, Ella G. Smith	1878-1942—wife of E.G.
1	Smith, Rosa M.	1885-1943—born in London
1	Smith, Mary	(no date)—Mother of Rev. Geo. E., born in Leeds
2	Smith, Francis Wetmore	1875-1937
2	Smith, Apollos A.	1825-1912
2	Smith, Lydia H. Martin	1834-1891—wife of A.A.
2	Smith, Phelps	1862-1937—son of A.A. & L.
2	Smith, Henry B. L.	1861-1891—son of A.A. & L.

Sec.		
2	Smith, Paul, Jr.	1870-1927—son of A.A. & L. (Buried at Woodlawn, N.Y.)
1	Sprague, Warren A.	1885-1923
1	Sprague, Mary Donovan	Aug. 24, 1880-Apr. 6, 1959—wife of Warren A.
1	Sprague, Richard	Jan. 17, 1912-Jan. 21, 1912—son of W. & M.
3	Sprague, Ethel G.	d Feb. 7, 1891—age 3 yrs., dau. of J.F. & A.C.
1	Stearns, Minnie M. Blanchard	1886-1909—wife of Wm. F.
2	Steenken, William	1876-1965
2	Steenken, Louise	1877-1957
2	Steenken, Gerald Edward	1942-1963
1	Steidl, John Henry (Dr.)	1899-1938
1	Sullivan, James	Feb. 19, 1878-July 18, 1954—2 Regt, Inf. NY NG WW I Pfc.
1	Sullivan, ...	1879-1944—his wife (James)
2	Sweet, Richard Allen	1923-1944—Pfc. 30th Inf. 3 D France, Africa
3	Sweet, David T.	1872-1948
3	Sweet, Mary M. Tyler	1873-1933—wife of David T.
3	Sweet, Marjorie F.	Dec. 15, 1918-Jan. 2, 1919
3	Sweet, Wyne Tyler	d July 21, 1908—age 12 yrs.
3	Sweet, Warren	d Jan. 27, 1904—age 5 mos., son of David & Mary
3	Sweet, Lemir	d July 5, 1902—age 1 yr., dau. of David & Mary
3	Sweet, David, Jr.	1911-1914
1	Taylor, Elizabeth S.	1905-1951
3	Tanner, James G.	d Feb. 22, 1871—age 41 yrs. Meb. Co. A 2nd NY Cav.
3	Tanner, Susan Hall	1842-1925—wife of James G.
3	Tanner, Libbie M.	d Apr. 15, 1886—age 17 yrs., dau. of James & Susan
1	Traynor, Harry	1887-1934
1	Traynor, Irene B.	1889-1924—wife of Harry
1	Traynor, Raymond Newell	1913-1944—Lt. USNR, Aviator WW II
3	Titus, William H.	1867-19....
3	Titus, Alta L. Hayes	1871-1932
3	Titus, William H.	Jan. 17, 1902-July 20, 1967—NY Tec 5 561 Sig. Air Wing BN WW II
3	Titus, James H.	May 16, 1877-July 14, 1945
3	Titus, Amy J. Otis	July 28, 1879-Dec. 28, 1966
1	Trudeau, Edward Livingston, Dr.	Oct. 5, 1848-Nov. 15, 1915
1	Trudeau, Francis Berger	1887-1956
1	Trudeau, Edw. Livingston, Jr.	d May 3, 1904—age 30 yrs., also a Dr.
1	Trudeau, Henry Berger	d 1878—age 8 mos.
1	Trudeau, Chatte B.	d Mar. 20, 1893—age 20 yrs.
1	Trudeau, Andrew J.	Apr. 25, 1907-July 23, 1930
2	Turner, Ella F.	1867-1941
3	Tyler, Gordon E.	1901-1958
3	Tyler, Willis W.	d Feb. 28, 1895—age 1 mo., son of Wortley & Lydia
3	Tyler, William Wortley	1870-1934
3	Tyler, Lydia Cross	1872-1948
3	Tyler, Milie L.	Oct. 3, 1899—age 10 yrs., son of Wortley & Lydia

2	Werner, Paul Avery	1903-1960
2	Wheeler, Oscar H.	1896-1951
2	Wheeler, Ruby Lyon	1897-1961—wife of Oscar
2	White, William Chapman	Feb. 20, 1903-Nov. 28, 1955
1	Wilcox, Claude E.	1877-1910
1	Wilcox, Ernest W.	1906-1944
1	Wilcox, Carrie M.	1880-1952
1	Wilcox, Alanson K.	d 1895—age 68 yrs. Pvt. Co. C, 118 Reg. NY Vol.
1	Wilcox, Sarah A.	d 1910—age 89 yrs., wife of A. K.
1	Wilcox, Sadie	(no date)—age 4 yrs. 8 mos. 8 days
3	Wiles, Lydia E.	1908-1939—wife of Ralph T.
3	Williams, Howard	1910-1954
3	Williams (infant)	d May22, 1935—of H. E. & N. M.

School Teachers
Town of Brighton

Nearly complete school attendance and grade records are on file in the vault at the Town Hall from 1871-1953.

SCHOOL DISTRICT No. 1 (Easy Street)

		No. in Class	
Melifsa Goodspeed	Nov. 20, 1871-Feb. 23, 1872	14	
	Apr. 29, 1872-Aug. 29, 1872	12	
Kattie Hewitt	Nov. 25, 1872-Mar. 11, 1873	13	
Eva Stoerrs	May 7, 1873-Aug. 8, 1873	12	$4 per week
	Nov. 12, 1873-Feb. 13, 1874	14	
Emma Toof	May 12, 1874-Aug. 21, 1874	14	
	May 3, 1875-Aug. 6, 1875	17	
Gertie Bartlett	Nov. 9, 1874-Feb. 13, 1875	23	
C. Louisa Will	Nov. 8, 1875-Mar. 17, 1876	16	$7.50 per week
	May 1, 1876-Aug. 4, 1876	14	$6 per week
Willie W. Smith	Dec. 1, 1879-Mar. 5, 1880	24	(from Jay)
Emeroy Bruce	Nov. 15, 1880-Mar. 2, 1881	18	
	Apr. 11, 1881-July 5, 1881	15	
Hattie Jorden	May 4, 1880-Aug. 6, 1880	14	
F. M. Noble	Nov. 14, 1881-Feb. 14, 1882	17	(from Bloom-
	Apr. 10, 1882-July 19, 1882	18	ingdale)
Carrie Noble	Nov. 10, 1884-Feb. 13, 1885	16	
Nellie M. Karapp	May 4, 1885-Aug. 7, 1885	11	
Lillian Macomber	Nov. 9, 1885-Feb. 19, 1886	24	
Hattie Duane	Apr. 19, 1886-July 23, 1886	18	
F. Noble	Nov. 11, 1889-Mar. 12, 1890	6	$8 per week
Halcyin Hutchins	Mar. 24, 1890-July 11, 1890	10	
Lottie Powell	Oct. 14, 1889-Jan. 31, 1890	7	
	Mar. 10, 1890-May 16, 1890	5	
	Oct. 12, 1890-Jan. 30, 1891	13	
Hattie Duane	Mar. 30, 1891-July 7, 1891	14	

		No. in Class	
Lottie Powell	Oct. 26, 1891-Mar. 18, 1892	14	
	Apr. 4, 1892 June 27, 1892	7	
Zoa Otis	Oct. 9, 1893-Jan. 26, 1894	11	
	Mar. 19, 1894-July 6, 1894	11	
Hattie Duane	Sept. 3, 1894-Dec. 21, 1894	13	
	Mar. 18, 1895-July 8, 1895	11	
	Sept. 21, 1896-Jan. 8, 1897	18	
	Mar. 22, 1897-July 9, 1897	23	
Julia Lenny	Sept. 23, 1901 for 32 wks	28	$9 per week
Eva Hamilton	Sept. 1902-May 1903	28	$10 per week
	Sept. 1903-June 1904	23	
Margaret Weir	Sept. 1904-June 1905	24	$10 per week
Evelena Fleming	Sept.-Dec. 1907	4	
Clair McCann	Jan. 1908-May 1908	16	$320 per yr.
	Sept. 1908-June 1909	5	
Netta Watson	Sept. 1909-May 1910	20	$336 per yr.
Cora McCasland	Sept. 1911-May 1912	24	$385 per yr.
Corabelle Elliot	Sept. 1912-June 1913	21	$408 per yr.
Anna Farrisee	Sept. 1914-June 1915	22	$468 per yr.
	Sept. 1915-June 1916	23	$432 per yr.
Mary Riley	Sept. 1917-June 1918	21	$600 per yr.
	Sept. 1920-June 1921	17	$1120 per yr.
Mrs. Robert Stevens	1921-1922	31	$1200 per yr.
	1922-1923	22	
Frances Webster Clark	1931-1932	24	$1500 per yr.

SCHOOL DISTRICT No. 2 (Keeses Mills)

Ann Goodspeed	Nov. 18, 1867-Feb. 21, 1868	16	
	May 4, 1868-Aug. 7, 1868	13	
Melifa Goodspeed	Nov. 23, 1868-Feb. 26, 1869	18	
Hattie Clark	May 10, 1869-Aug. 20, 1869	15	
Anna M. Scanlin	Oct. 17, 1892-Feb. 15, 1893	28	$128 for term
Jennie Kibbe	Mar. 13, 1893-June 30, 1893	19	
Ida O'Dwyer	Sept. 8, 1902-Dec. 19, 1902	35	
	Mar. 2, 1909-June 26, 1903	19	
Julia McCarthy	Sept. 1908-June 1909	29	$416 per yr.
Elizabeth Sullivan	Sept. 1910-June 1911	24	each did part of
Nettie Sullivan			the year
Katherine McCarthy	Sept. 1912-Jan. 1913		
Theresa McCarthy	Feb. 1913-June 1913	25	
	Sept. 1913-June 1914	38	$56 per month
	Sept. 1916-June 1917	14	$600 per yr.
Ellen Leary	Sept. 1917-June 1918		
Katherine McCarthy	Sept. 1917-June 1918		
Ellen Leary	Sept. 1918-June 1919	43	$700 per yr.
Daisy E. Otis	Sept. 1918-June 1919		$700 per yr.
Ellen Leary	Sept. 1919-June 1920	38	$900 per yr.
Olga Etienne	Sept. 1919-June 1920		
	Sept. 1920-June 1921	17	$1050 per yr.
	Sept. 1921-June 1922	22	
Daisy O. McDermid	Sept. 1921-June 1922	37	
Olga Etienne	Sept. 1922 June 1923	28	
Frances Webster	Sept. 1922-June 1923	43	
Catherine Benham	Sept. 1924-June 1925	30	$1200 per yr.
Emma Rooney	Sept. 1924-June 1925		$1200 per qr.

SCHOOL DISTRICT No. 3 (McColloms)

		No. in Class	
Gladys McArthur ⎫	1909-1910—all three	10	
Margaret Robbins ⎬	shared school year		
Katie Sullivan ⎭			
Hazel Cohn	1914-1915	8	
Pearle N. Beyerl	1915-1916		$378
	1916-1917		
Mrs. Robert Stevens	1917-1918	8	$600 per yr.
	1918-1919	7	$665 per yr.
Nettie Selkirk	1919-1920	9	$800 per yr.
	1920-1921	8	
	1921-1922	6	$1000 per yr.
	1922-1923	4	$1000 per yr.
	1923-1924	7	$900 per yr.
	1924-1925	5	$900 per yr.

SCHOOL DISTRICT No. 4 (Gabriels and Rainbow)

Amanda Avery	Dec. 12, 1870-Mar. 24, 1871	14	
Mary Pranae	July 10, 1871-Sept. 18, 1871	14	
Ella Storrs	Nov. 2, 1871-Aug. 8, 1873	18	
	Nov. 10, 1873-Feb. 3, 1874	18	
	May 18, 1874-Aug. 14, 1874	11	
Selina Beaudry	Nov. 1872-Feb. 1873	18	
Gertie Bartlett	Nov. 1874-Feb. 1875		
Emma Toof	Nov. 16 ,1874-Feb. 19, 1875		
Maggie Ricketson	Nov. 16, 1874-Feb. 19, 1875	6	$5/wk., age 78
Ella Carpenter	May 1875-Aug. 1875	14	
Emma Hough	Dec. 6, 1875-Mar. 10, 1876	22	
Carrie Weller	May 7, 1876-Aug. 16, 1876	6	
Fannie Works	Nov. 20, 1876-Feb. 25, 1877	22	
Nellie M. Hoff	April and May, 1877	15	
Laura Miller	May 21, 1877-Aug. 17, 1877	20	$64/term, age 16
Eldridge Ricketson	Nov. 26, 1877-Mar. 15, 1878	24	
Laura Miller	May 13, 1878-Aug. 8, 1878	20	
Mrs. Geo. Hewitt	Dec. 1, 1879-Mar. 5, 1880	17	
Kittie Brown	May 11, 1880-Aug. 12, 1880	17	
Mary Lamson	Nov. 7, 1881-Feb. 11, 1882	17	
Addie Wardner	Nov. 7, 1881-Feb. 17, 1882	4	
Sarah Parklin	May 1, 1882-Aug. 4, 1882	14	
Jennie Winch	May 1, 1882-Aug. 4, 1882	4	
F. A. Noble	Nov. 6, 1882-Feb. 13, 1883	14	
A. J. Harlow	May 7, 1883-Aug. 10, 1883	13	
James Wardner	Nov. 13, 1882-June 4, 1883	5	(Rainbow Br'ch)
Addie Wardner	Oct. 29, 1883-May 4, 1884	3	(Rainbow Br'ch)
F. A. Noble	Nov. 12, 1883-Feb. 15, 1884	11	
	Apr. 28, 1884-Aug. 4, 1884	7	
Addie Wardner	Oct. 14, 1884-Apr. 18, 1885	3	
Abbie Harlow	Oct. 27, 1884-Jan. 30, 1885	12	
Lillian Maccomber	May 5, 1885-Aug. 18, 1885	18	
	Nov. 7, 1887-Feb. 10, 1888	4	
Lydia Maccomber	Nov. 7, 1887-Feb. 10, 1888	13	
	Oct. 1, 1888-Jan. 4, 1889	15	
Carrie Pierce	Apr. 29, 1888-Aug. 7, 1888	11	
Addie Wardner	Oct. 1, 1888-Apr. 27, 1889	2	$3 per week

		No. in Class	
Kittie Wardner	Oct. 8, 1890-May 1, 1891	4	
Agnes Brand	Oct. 14, 1889-Jan. 31, 1890	13	
	Mar. 17, 1890-July 4, 1890	15	
	Sept. 8, 1890-Jan. 23, 1891	13	
Madge Dustin	Apr. 28, 1891-July 10, 1891	9	
Kittie Wardner	Sept. 28, 1891-May 6, 1892	5	(Rainbow Br'ch)
Mary Carroll	Aug. 31, 1891-Jan. 20, 1892	20	
W. G. Cushman	Mar. 28, 1892-July 22, 1892	23	
Hattie Duane	Sept. 25, 1893-Dec. 29, 1893	31	
Lelitia Young	Mar. 12, 1894-July 27, 1894	41	$7.50 per week
Willis McCasland	Sept. 17, 1894-Feb. 15, 1895	44	$9 per week
Frank Weston	Sept. 23, 1895-Jan. 15, 1896	46	
Alice Carter	Mar. 25, 1895-July 12, 1895	43	$7.50 per week
	Mar. 16, 1896-July 10, 1896	41	
	Sept. 14, 1896-Jan. 13, 1897	39	
Nettie Wilkins	Mar. 1, 1897-June 8, 1897	40	$9 per week
	Sept. 13, 1897-Jan. 12, 1898	40	
	Mar. 15, 1898-June 1, 1898	34	
Katherine Tack	Sept. 12, 1898-Jan. 27, 1899	35	$160 for term
	Mar. 20, 1899-July 19, 1899	14	
F. G. Harrington	Sept. 11, 1899-Jan. 4, 1900	51	
Mary Flanagan	Sept. 17, 1900-June 7, 1601	29	$320 for term
Anna McCarthy	Oct. 21, 1901-Feb. 28, 1902	29	$11 per week
	Mar. 3, 1902-June 23, 1902		
Elizabeth McCarthy	Oct. 21, 1901-Feb. 28, 1902	34	$9 per week
	Sept. 8, 1902-June 5, 1903	38	$320 for term
	Sept. 7, 1903-May 27, 1904	42	$320 for term
Isabel Flanagan	Sept. 1902-June 1903	31	$320 per year
Mary Flanagan	Sept. 1903-June 1904	26	$320 per year
Hannah Sullivan	Sept. 1906-June 1907	32	$336 per year
	Sept. 1907-June 1908	37	$352 per year
Martha Weir	Sept. 1906-June 1907	33	$336 per year
Katherine Murphy	Sept. 1907-June 1908	29	
Mildred Hall	Sept. 1908-June 1909	33	
J. Earl Brennan	Sept. 1908-June 1909		
Lena McCarthy	Sept. 1909-June 1910	40	$352 per year
Nellie Downs	Sept. 1909-June 1910		$352 per year
Nellie Downs	Sept. 1910-June 1911	38	$440 per year
Lena McCarthy	Sept. 1910-June 1911	28	$440 per year
Nellie Downs	Sept. 1911-May 1912	35	$352 per year
Maude Bush	Sept. 1911-May 1912	26	$384 per year
Dennis Adams	Sept. 1912-June 1913	31	$440 per year
Anna Farrisee	Sept. 1916-June 1917	20	

From this point on it was a three-room school with a teacher in each room, part of the time.

1917-1918	Daisy Otis, Nellie Downs Mac-Donald, Anna Farrisee	$600 a year
1919-1920	Ellen Leary, Olga Etienne	
1922-1923	Eunice Boyce, Vivian Bigelow	
1923-1924	Abbie Boswell, Nellie MacDonald	
1924-1925	Abbie Boswell, Nellie MacDonald	

1925-1926	Abbie Boswell, Nellie MacDonald and Nettie Selkirk
1926-1927	Nettie Selkirk, Gertrude Downs, Anabel Lemieux, Abbie Martin
1927-1928	Nettie Selkirk, Anabel Lemieux, Gertrude Downs
1928-1929	Frances Sullivan, Gertrude Downs, Nettie Selkirk, Reginald Russell
1929-1930	Frances Sullivan, Gertrude Downs, Reginald Russell, and Mary Ann Gratto
1930-1931	Mary Gratto, Frances Sullivan, Gertrude Downs, Marion Handlin
1931-1932	Mary Gratto, Reginald Russell, Gertrude Downs, Marion Handlin
1932-1940	Mary Gratto, Reginald Russell, Gert Downs Otis, Marion Handlin
1940-1941	Gertrude Otis, Reginald Russell, Marion Brewster, Marjorie Gillespie
1941-1942	Reginald Russell, Marjorie Gillespie, Hope Augustine, Sarah Arnold and Mary Arnold
1942-1943	Olga Faulkner, Nellie Fletcher, Eleanor Morrison, Linda DelBel
1943-1944	Nellie Fletcher, Nellie Thawaits, Greta Mathews, Linda Del Bel
1944-1945	Nellie Thawaits, Bernice McGowan
1945-1948	Frances Bunker, Bernice McGowan. Helen Stacy
1948-1950	Helen Stacy, Frances Bunker, Ursula Murphy
1950-1951	Frances Bunker
1951-1953	Frances Bunker, Pearl LeValley, Phyllis Tyler

INDEX

202

Bibliography

Beers, D. G.—*Atlas of Franklin County*. Phila., Pa., 1876.
Brighton Town Records—school registers, minutes of board, war records, etc.
Cook, Mac—Camp Lou. *Harper's New Monthly Magazine*, May 1881.
Donaldson, Alfred L.—*History of the Adirondacks*. N.Y., Century. c 1921.
Forest Leaves Magazine—Gabriels Sanitorium, 1903-1907.
Gabriels Sanitorium folders and reports.
History of Clinton and Franklin Counties—J. W. Lewis Co. 1880.
Hotel folders from Rainbow Inn, Brighton, Garondah, Paul Smith's Hotel, Clark Wardner Camps.
Landon, Harry F.—*History of the North Country*. Historical Pub. Co., 1932.
Longstreth, T. Morris—*The Adirondacks*. N.Y., Century Press. c 1919.
Lusk, Rev. William B., St. Regis Presbyterian Church, Paul Smiths, N. Y., n.d.
Murray, William H. H.—*Adventures in the Wilderness*. Bost., Copples and Hurd, 1869.
New York Central Railroad. Map and folder on Adirondacks, 1912-1916.
New York State Forest, Fish and Game Reports. Various years.
Paul Smiths' College Catalog, 1942-1970.
Rainbow Sanitorium folders.
Rider, Edward—*Franklin County in the World War*. n.d. (1918?)
Scrapbooks of newspaper clippings loaned by Earl McArthur, Gladys Blanchard, and Saranac Lake Public Library.
Seaver, Frederick J.—*Historical Sketches of Franklin County*. Albany, J. B. Lyon, c 1918.
Smith, Phelps—Personal papers in Paul Smith's College Library.
Stoddard, S. R.—*The Adirondacks*. Pub. by the author, various editions.
Taped recordings of personal interviews with Mr. and Mrs. Orman Doty and Arthur Leavitt.
Titus, John H.—*Adirondack Pioneers*. Troy Times Press, 1899.
Trudeau, Edward Livingston—*An Autobiography*. Garden City, Doubleday Page, c 1915.
Wallace, Edwin R.—*Descriptive Guide to Adirondacks*. Syracuse, 1894.

Almost every old-time resident of the town has, at one time or another, talked with me about their recollections. Special mention to Walter and Milly Wardner, Halsey and Florence Bruellia, Gladys Blanchard, Matthew Knudson, Mae Hogan, and the Orman Doty family.

204